Dyslexia

Learning Disorder or Creative Gift?

Dyslexia

Learning Disorder or Creative Gift?

Cornelia Jantzen

Floris Books

Translated by Matthew Barton

First published in German by Verlag Uracchaus in 2000
2nd edition 2004
First published in English by Floris Books in 2009

British CIP Data available

ISBN 978-086315-709-7

Printed in Great Britain
By Athenaeum Press Ltd., Gateshead.

Contents

Part III ... And now for some kind of connecting bridge

Appendices

Preface

'I was constantly afraid that people might find out I wasn't a proper person, that I was handicapped.'

There could scarcely be a clearer, more shocking indictment of the effects on a child of traditional verdicts about dyslexics: as people incapable of learning, low in intelligence and defective.

Cornelia Jantzen's book gives a striking account of how she overcame this common, narrowly prejudiced view of dyslexia. Through daily observations, encounters and experiences, she involves us in a process that gives greater insight into the special mode of perception and thinking of dyslexic children.

In this project two people above all are exemplary for her: Ronald Davis, whose method teaches how the apparent hindrances suffered by dyslexic children can be overcome through their own underlying gifts; and Rudolf Steiner, whose ideas on education at the beginning of the twentieth century showed how *every* child can develop in an integrated and holistic way. Cornelia Jantzen details thoughts of Steiner's that helped her to recognize and nurture the special gifts of dyslexic children.

The moving thing about this book is the author's deep regard for dyslexic children, her sympathy with their suffering, her courage in breaking away from fixed judgements and in seeking to understand a so often misinterpreted reality in order to offer help.

Drawing on the Davis method and Rudolf Steiner's educational ideas, Cornelia Jantzen conveys above all a joy in discovery and a courage for meeting contemporary phenomena in the spirit of open-minded enquiry. May it inspire us — for that is precisely what we need today.

Felicitas Vogt

A proper book needs an introduction

So now it's grown into a book ...

It started with Post-its full of notes, quickly recorded experiences with my own and other children, with many questions and next to no answers about the phenomenon of dyslexia. The subject was one which had interested me academically over twenty years before, but had faded from my view — until, with vivid immediacy, it caught up with me again in duplicate, in the shape of my own children sitting there in front of me at the breakfast table.

Thus began an exciting time of discovery, rethinking and learning — and also, to my great good fortune, of new acquaintances. Alongside many other people who enriched my life, I met Ronald Davis, who recurs a great deal in this book; and (though I'm not sure that I can say this, yet for me personally it's true) I got to know Rudolf Steiner, who died in 1925 but who lives on vitally today in his works, ideas, visions, in his view of the human being and his educational ideas.

Davis and Steiner were the two essential and revolutionary figures who I would never have encountered if the phenomenon of dyslexia had not seated itself unexpectedly at my breakfast table. Drawing on them and my own experience, recorded in that pile of Post-its, in 1997 I produced a photocopied and self-published brochure entitled 'How we've been maltreated ...' which forms Part I of this book.

And in the spring of 2000, with two new parts added, it grew into a book, a proper book. But is it 'finished?' Of course not! I'm still miles away from thinking every thought to its final conclusion, solving every problem, answering every question. You'll need to know this before you go any further. However finished it may look, it makes absolutely no claim to completeness.

Please read and regard it in the same way that it gradually formed and developed over about two years: as a kind of puzzle to which still, almost daily, new pieces are added — both from the literature on the subject, where I keep discovering new aspects and perspectives, and from daily life and practical experiences in my work with dyslexic children and adolescents. I have recorded a process of development here, and its goal still lies in the future. This is a stock-take, therefore, and not a final audit.

You will see that the book contains many detailed quotations, for I want to convey all the 'parts of the puzzle' in as authentic a way as possible, and thus place the ideas of those quoted alongside each other as objectively as I can, as food for debate. At the same time I am aware that subjective colourings from my own way of thinking cannot be denied. For this reason I urge you to read the quotations and suggestions I cite in their original context — particularly if they strike you as 'unbelievable.'

My first, key part of the puzzle was to read the book by Ronald Davis: *The Gift of Dyslexia: Why Some of the Brightest People Can't Read ... and How They Can Learn*. I found it difficult to understand the change of paradigm from a 'disability' to a 'talent' or 'gift,' or even to begin to accept it. That is why I understand the fact that this view of dyslexia and the resulting methods for overcoming it are still the subject of fierce debate.

This is also, after all, why I wrote this book. In daily life I repeatedly tested my many doubts and my lack of understanding, and continually found that the insights underlying the Davis approach were affirmed. At the same time, it should not be forgotten that implementing the Davis method in practice is not exactly straightforward; it is not easy to integrate mastering symbols by visualizing them into learning methods and schools. Children must maintain their motivation to use the Davis method, so we keep in touch with pupils and parents after the consultation week. In the appendix you will find further information about this, along with the report of a mother's experiences, interviews with dyslexic children and adolescents, and an interview with a certified Davis adviser.

I am not concerned here with methods of handling or even curing dyslexia, but rather with developing an understanding for the special modes of perception and thinking which underlie it, and are the basis of dyslexics' special gifts. I want to work my way through to this understanding with you, at the same time showing the correlations between particular dyslexic gifts and Rudolf Steiner's visionary approach to education. Here, I am convinced, lies the key to hitherto untapped possibilities for successful acquisition of literacy skills.

The ideas and suggestions in my book are therefore intended for all:

- who are curious and willing to engage with new ideas and do not expect any sure-fire remedy;
- who are still wondering about the 'dyslexia' phenomenon or other 'learning disabilities' and have no easy answers;
- who harbour mild doubts about today's school learning, whether in mainstream schools or Waldorf schools;
- who are involved with primary-level literacy teaching;
- who have always considered Rudolf Steiner's educational ideas to be innovative;
- who are fascinated by the huge diversity in human modes of perception;

- who are keen to attempt to learn more about the nature of genius;
- parents, teachers and therapists, who put great effort into helping children with 'learning disabilities';
- dyslexics, old and young, to whom I owe so much.

My unbounded sympathy goes out to all the above. I have written this book for them. And with them I want to carry on trying things out, thinking and investigating.

Cornelia Jantzen
Hamburg, March 2000

Foreword to the second edition

I referred to the first edition of this book as 'unfinished,' but the second makes no claim, either, to being complete. However, in the past four years I have naturally carried on working and learning. Working with dyslexic children and teenagers continues to be an ever new and wonderful experience. Much has happened in the intervening period. With a qualified psychologist I founded the Leonardo Learning Studio in Hamburg, where we advise and consult on dyslexia, numeracy problems, ADD/ADHD and handwriting difficulties. We hold support discussions with parents and teachers, and give lectures and workshops in teacher-training institutes, schools and nursery schools to promote understanding for these special children. On a few occasions I have also run external consultation weeks. Mutually supportive work is currently ongoing, for example, with a state-funded Waldorf school in Germany.

As a result of to my daughter's six-month stay in Cape Town and a friendship that developed with a support teacher at a Waldorf school in Johannesburg, I established an interesting connection with South African Waldorf schools. During a consultation week in Cape Town, a lovely text was created (in English, of course) which I have added to the appendix (*see* p.177).

Less lovely are the developments in recent years relating to dyslexic children within the German school system. PISA (Programme for International Student Assessment) and IGLU (Internationale Grundschul-Lese-Untersuching/ International Reading Literacy Study) are currently leading to education policies which allow children ever less scope for development. Early schooling and continual achievement testing in literacy and numeracy leave little room for dyslexics to develop their innate capabilities. Pupils and parents are subject to ever-increasing pressure and, primarily in mainstream schools, are quickly primed for failure.

In contrast, there is an increasing call in the USA for a focus on overall, holistic development. In 2003, an article appeared in the Dyslexia Association International's *Dyslexic Reader* by Professor David Elkind, professor of child development at Tufts University and the author of *Reinventing Childhood* and *The Hurried Child*. He highlights in particular how important it is for children to learn through interest and tangible sensory experience, and that early academic training does not pay off. He cites great figures in education such as Froebel, Montessori, Steiner and Vygotsky.

In the field of brain research, meanwhile, it has been found that dyslexics can read better by using alternative strategies, even leading to better reading competency (see the bibliography for a list of related articles). Particularly important here is teaching not only the sound but also the meaning of the word when reading.

In Iceland, a dream is in the process of becoming reality. In the next three years all schools in the country are to start using the Davis Learning Strategies. In 2003, Ronald Davis's book *The Gift of Learning* was number two on Iceland's bestseller list, just behind Harry Potter. (In passing I'll mention that many of my pupils from three years ago, whose texts are printed in the appendix, have become Harry Potter bookworms!)

Back in Germany, I am particularly disturbed by the increasing medication of children with Ritalin. Far from being prescribed only for extreme fidgets, this drug is now given to all who 'can't concentrate properly.' I consider it highly dubious to give children behaviour-altering drugs and would here like to suggest alternative approaches such as those found in the books below.

The new book by Ronald Davis, *The Gift of Learning*, offers specific practical approaches to ADD, dyscalculia and handwriting problems.

Another approach to special children can be found in:

Georg Kühlewind, *Star Children*, Temple Lodge, 2004.

Lee Carroll & Jan Tober, *The Indigo Children*, Hay House, 1999.*

The following book contains many practical suggestions, especially for dyslexics:

Jeffrey Freed & Laurie Parsons, *Right-Brained Children in a Left-Brained World*, Prentice Hall & IBD, 1998

And finally, I found welcome support for parents in Barbara Coloroso's book, *Kids Are Worth It*, Somerville House Books, 1998

'... because they are children, and for no other reason, they have dignity and value, simply because they exist ...'

BARBARA COLOROSO

Cornelia Jantzen
Hamburg, spring 2004

---

*   And in the following German books: Henning Köhler: *War Michel aus Lönneberga aufmerksamkeitsgestört?* Verlag Freies Geistesleben, Stuttgart, 2002.
Gerald Hüther / Helmut Bonney: *Neues vom Zappelphilipp* Walter Verlag, Düsseldorf, 2002.
Thom Hartmann: *Eine andere Art, die Welt zu sehen.* ADS Verlag Schmidt-Römhild, Lübeck, 2003.

'Someone who desired to understand everything about me would find harmony where, since he does not understand me, he sees only contradiction.'

RUDOLF STEINER, IN A LETTER (1903)

Part I

How we've been maltreated ...

The Phenomenon of Dyslexia

Dyslexics are, ostensibly, people who have difficulty in learning, and later using, written language. Some remain more or less illiterate while others learn to cope with their disability.

There are countless publications on this phenomenon, a flood of efforts to explain the supposed causes, and even more suggestions for treating it. But they so far add up to the realization that 'learning to live with it' is the only remedy 'possible for dyslexics. This may sound drastic, but most dyslexics can cope outstandingly well with the last residues of their dyslexia (bad spelling, slow or imprecise reading).'[1]

In my view, however, the above is not accurate for 'most' but only a fraction of those affected. Many despair in advance, are shunted off to special schools and end up unemployed and hopeless; some even end up as criminals.

The social stigmatization attached to the inability to adequately master a decisive 'cultural technique' often gives dyslexics a negative self-image, despite or even because of well-meaning therapies to which they are usually subjected:

Almost all children and adolescents who underwent dyslexia therapy, with all the pre, post and ongoing testing this involves, showed general traits of increased anxiety, feelings of inferiority, lack of self-confidence, uncertainty and a distorted self-image. [2]

This feeling of failing to meet acknowledged standards can be expressed in many different ways. The following passage appeared in the *Frankfurter Rundschau* newspaper on August 4, 1997:

'Always looking for new excuses is much worse than this here,' said Karl-Heinz. By 'this here' he meant reading and writing. Karl-Heinz is 53. Until a few years ago, letters for him were nothing more than a jumble of signs on paper, and his ability to decipher

them was 'just about non-existent.' He always had to think up excuses like forgetting his glasses, so that no one would notice his difficulty ...

In his personal life he has achieved a good deal. He married, became a father and later built his own house. Nevertheless, his reading and writing difficulties have been an enormous burden — so much so that this expressed itself in physical symptoms and he became ill. 'The worst of it is that one feels held back and excluded if one can't read.' Does he still fear that someone will notice his illiteracy? 'Yes, every day!'

The following is a Christmas wish list composed by a twelve-year-old girl:

Wishis

Bicycel   Camara
LEGO   Stams
SPace (statiern)
abel to read

                                           WWF

In a report on a girl in Grade Six (age eleven/twelve) at a German comprehensive mainstream school, a school psychologist states:

For psychological reasons I support suspending obligatory school attendance for Sarah [name altered]. Sarah is a pronounced dyslexic of high intelligence, who makes great demands on herself. Since she cannot fulfil these demands due to her partial learning disorder, she refuses school altogether.

This application was not granted however.

In an interview published in the magazine *Ab 40* (*After 40*), a dyslexic answered as follows to a reporter who asked him, 'Were you ashamed?'

Oh yes! I was constantly afraid that people might find out I wasn't a proper person, that I was handicapped ... [Perhaps not all dyslexics] feel so cornered as I did, but — psychologically and in their feelings — they are certainly also up against it. The perception they have of themselves, and their feelings and self-esteem, are very destructive ...

This can lead to complete despair:

'When Siegfried died it was a shock for all of us,' recalls Renate Hackethal. Twelve years after the death of the dyslexic blonde boy from the North Sea island of Föhr, this special-school teacher is still perturbed about it.

For years she practised reading and writing with him, accompanying him through his disappointments at secondary school, through to the start of a promising career as a mechanical engineer.

But just a few days before the professors at Dortmund University could congratulate the 32-year-old on his brilliant exam results, he was found dead on his bed. [3]

'Learning to live' with dyslexia, without understanding what is wrong with you compared with everyone else, makes for an uphill struggle. Why do people struggle to understand you, even though you yourself see things so clearly? (a feeling that dyslexics repeatedly express); and secondly, what has caused this 'disability' and how on earth can it be overcome?

Solving the Riddle of Dyslexia

In 1980, the American Ronald Davis discovered how his own dyslexia functioned and how it could successfully be overcome. Fourteen years later, after intensive further research following experiments on himself, he was able to formulate his findings in the following spectacular sentence: 'The mental function that causes dyslexia is a gift in the truest sense of the word: a natural ability, a talent. It is something special that enhances the individual.' [4]

This sounds incredible, but it gives us an inkling, for the first time, why so many famous historical and contemporary individuals clearly had or have dyslexic disorders. They include: Thomas A. Edison, Albert Einstein, Alfred Hitchcock, Agatha Christie, John F. Kennedy, Winston Churchill, Paul Ehrlich, Paganini, Leonardo da Vinci, Walt Disney, Nelson Rockefeller, Charles Darwin, Ernest Hemingway, Francois Mitterand, Carl Gustav of Sweden, Carl Lewis, Whoopie Goldberg, Cher, John Lennon, Tom Cruise and many more.

The following is reported of Leonardo da Vinci:

The first target at which Leonardo's polemic aims is poetry, i.e. literature, which he puts in the dock. And with his complaint against it he simultaneously defends himself, for he admits his failings. The painter is 'not well-read'; he has not fully mastered the literary tools of the time, and knows that he 'cannot express himself well' and therefore also cannot read and quote from the great volumes of humanity. [5]

Ronald Davis comments:

Having dyslexia won't make every dyslexic a genius, but it is good for the self-esteem of all dyslexics to know their minds work in exactly the same way as the minds of great geniuses ... Here are the basic abilities all dyslexics share:

1. *They can utilize the brain's ability to alter and create perceptions (the primary ability)*
2. *They are highly aware of the environment*
3. *They are more curious than average*
4. *They think mainly in pictures instead of words*
5. *They are highly intuitive and insightful*
6. *They think and perceive multi-dimensionally (using all the senses)*
7. *They can experience thought as reality*
8. *They have vivid imaginations*

These eight basic abilities, if not suppressed, invalidated or destroyed by parents or the educational process, will result in two characteristics: higher than normal intelligence and extraordinary creative abilities. From these the true gift of dyslexia can emerge — the gift of mastery. [6]

Dyslexia as 'gift of mastery.' How can we use such a sentence, such an insight, when we are much more likely to see frustrated children and adolescents facing a jumble of letters in despair? I have been preoccupied with this discrepancy and the riddle of dyslexia for over twenty years now: it started during my studies, deepened as I worked on my education dissertation, and continues to this day in my daily work with dyslexic children, two of whom are my own. (My middle daughter, however, is not dyslexic.)

In fact I always sensed a discrepancy between observations of 'learning disorders' or 'literacy problems' (or whatever the 'disability' happened to be called at the time) and the simultaneous observation of something strikingly different, which to begin with I could not identify at all, and certainly would not have called the 'gift of mastery.'

The other thing was nameless — but it existed.

Ronald Davis's insights are actually least surprising of all to parents of dyslexic children; and it is therefore no wonder that many mothers or fathers of such children attend his workshops. Of course one might assume that it simply enhances the self-esteem of participants to persuade themselves that their kids are, in reality, child prodigies. But this is not what it is about at all. Of course they are not prodigies, although they are certainly intelligent, as can easily be proven with any intelligence test.

It is much more a question of a different kind of thinking, of often strange cognitive processes and ways of seeing that are alien to us, with which these children approach daily life. Also, above and beyond this, 'spiritual things' that astonish us, and which we can't classify.

Davis's book and his workshops enabled me for the first time to bring my divergent observations of dyslexia together into a harmonious whole, in which all the pieces of the puzzle fitted.

Over the years my personal experiences with dyslexics — long before I was aware of the book by Ronald Davis, which only appeared in 1995 — were augmented by a quite different observation, which was initially more of an inkling, a hunch.

It began when my children were attending a Steiner-Waldorf school and, in consequently, I gradually encountered a new world of ideas and images. More and more frequently, in fact, I discovered a striking correlation between the basic ideas of Waldorf education and the often curious perspectives and modes of thinking of my dyslexic children — outlooks that they had always possessed and which had surprised me long before they went to the Waldorf school. Our home, it has to be said, was not anthroposophical in outlook.

I do not know whether others had discovered this correlation previously, maybe because they had developed a deeper understanding of anthroposophy. Nevertheless, while my eldest was still playing in her sandpit, many of my friends commented that this was definitely a child for the Waldorf school! Why this was so I did not know at the time.

My eldest initially went to the local primary school, until it no longer worked and her pain threshold was reached and exceeded. Then it seemed right: yes, she was a child for the Waldorf school. This was increasingly confirmed in subsequent years as I gained greater insight into Waldorf education, and my inklings of a 'relatedness' between anthroposophy and dyslexia became more tangible. But as far as writing and reading are concerned, she still has great difficulties, as does my youngest, who went straight to the Waldorf school without the detour through mainstream schooling.

Where does the contradiction lie here, and where the plausibility?

In my experience of my children's schooling the answer to this question remained hidden to me however much the various teachers and therapists worked to help them. I have absolutely no wish to criticize any of them, but I was sensitized by Ronald Davis's findings and insights, and went on a quest for the key to the origins of anthroposophy.

Rudolf Steiner — A Dyslexic?

Maybe the answer lies with him, that thinker of genius who in so many ways was ahead of his time (and ours too). We know a lot about him, but how well do we know him? He said of himself that as an eight-year-old he misspelt every word, and at fourteen or fifteen he could not write properly.

Why was it so difficult for Rudolf Steiner to learn this technique, particularly as in those days much more time in school was spent teaching reading and writing? The answer lies in the special ways in which dyslexia works and its closeness to genius. I shall expand on this, beginning with a — for me key — quotation:

We read books; here we find meaningful contents conveyed by little signs that we designate a, b, c, etc. We do not consider how we were maltreated in learning these signs, for they have no relationship whatever with our inner life. [7]

Drawing on Ronald Davis's findings and phenomenal parallels in the books and lectures by Rudolf Steiner, I would now like to look beyond functionality to see why the world of letters has no relation to the inner world of the dyslexic.

I will make use of quotations so that everyone can form a picture for himself of the correspondences that strike me so forcefully. Naturally I will have to limit myself to a few; but there are endless further quotations that fit with the picture. Now and then I will give longer quotes, since it is important to me that all comments can be placed in context. At the same time, though, I'm faced with the problem of managing this 'dialogue,' for I am trying to give logical order to something that cannot be grasped by logic alone; the thinking of the authors quoted is so confusingly multi-layered. No doubt we could only understand them fully if we also had the gift of observing everything simultaneously.

At the time of writing, the only available texts by Ronald Davis were *The Gift of Dyslexia*, his seminar handbook and my personal notes from workshops.

From the wealth of Steiner's writings, on the other hand, I will initially limit myself to quotations from ten of his works, mostly transcripts of his lectures. *

---

*   In the meantime, I have read additional texts and lectures by Rudolf Steiner and found many more parallels. In what follows I will not cite these passages, but will refer to them. Interested readers can then seek them out in the corresponding volumes of the Complete Edition (GA numbers. See bibliography.) And if it is somewhat audacious to summarize a whole tendency of thought after such limited reading — well, then I shall be audacious.

Multi-level Thinking

Ronald Davis describes three characteristics common to all dyslexics:

1. The capacity to form pictorial concepts, i.e. to think in mental images.
2. The capacity to 'register' a mental image as though it were an actual perception.
3. A lower than average confusion threshold.

All three characteristics are in continual mutual interplay.

As an infant, the dyslexic already develops the first two into a highly effective method for resolving suddenly arising 'confusion' (the word Davis uses), such as lack of clarity, perplexity or indecision in identifying objects unfamiliar to him:

In an attempt to resolve confusion, the process of pictorial concept formation kicks in automatically, and the unrecognized object is formed into a concept from possibly several hundred different points of view. In a confused state, these mental images are regarded by the mind and absorbed by the memory as if they were actual observations. However useful these images may be in identifying objects, they are imaginary and therefore false sense perceptions ...

During this time the person is disorientated, and the length of such disorientation can either be indeterminate or last for a few minutes or hours. The senses impaired and altered by this activity are sight, hearing, balance, movement and the sense of time ...

If this process leads to precise recognition, the confusion is resolved, together with the threshold of confusion, and the disorientation has either only small consequences or none. In certain creative and physical activities, it can in fact be very useful and advantageous, as one can see with many dyslexic inventors, athletes and artists. [8]

The 'sense organ' by means of which the dyslexic observes unknown objects 'from possibly several hundred different points of view' is what Ronald Davis calls 'the mind's eye.' He comments on this:

> *The mind's eye does have a location. In fact, it has a multitude of possible locations. It is wherever its owner intends it, wishes it or perceives it to be. If this sounds like a supernatural or metaphysical concept, please remember that dyslexics are able to experience their mental images as actual perceptions. So if they place the mind's eye in a particular place, they gain the ability to experience their perceptions from that perspective.* [9]

One could also put it like this: in the state of 'disorientation' (I will return to this term later; it is possible that 'de-orientation' would be more precise) the dyslexic looks with his mind's eye at what has confused him and, by circling round it with this mind's eye, he arrives at an altered perception in the real world. At the same time, though, this quickly leads him to recognize the stimulus that confused him.

Ronald Davis is no doubt aware that his terms 'confusion,' 'disorientation' and even 'mind's eye' represent a balancing act between the physical and metaphysical world, thus exposing him almost inevitably to criticism that what he says cannot be proven. On the other hand, he himself is the proof. Thus he asks and answers simultaneously:

> *Is the person having an out-of-body experience? Or is the person's mind manufacturing the perceptual stimuli needed to make these multiple views? I really don't know. I just know it happens.* [10]

Over 70 years ago, Rudolf Steiner spoke thus of the 'spiritual eye:'

> *When we move in the world, seeing with the eye of soul but leaving our physical eyes behind; when, in other words, we leave our corporeality via the eye, we enter the region where imagination reigns.* [11]

and:

> *Thus you can see that imaginative thinking addresses the whole human being, and that the whole person must live in such imaginative knowledge. In the case of higher vision this is greatly intensified.*

Now you don't need to be surprised that knowledge or insight gained by such means addresses and concerns the whole human being. But then one also notices that much in the world is different from what is perceptible for our external senses. And above all one finds that it is possible to live in a world in which space no longer has any importance ...

In imaginative knowledge, however, the spatial dimension gradually ceases altogether. Everything becomes temporal. In the imaginative realm, time has the same significance as space does in the physical world. And this now leads to something else — to an insight that time really has an enduring quality, that it in fact endures. [12]

It is difficult for us to understand this with our predominantly analytic and logically trained mode of thinking. I will therefore look more closely at the 'dyslexic characteristics' and their associated concepts. First I'd like to return to the second of these: registering a mental image as though it were an actual perception. To be able to do this, the dyslexic uses the capacity of disorientation, that is:

Loss of one's position or direction in relation to other things; a state of mind in which mental perceptions do not agree with the true facts and conditions in the environment; in some people this is an automatic response to confusion. People who disorientate easily sometimes feel dizzy. [13]

We are familiar with something like this from common daily situations. For example, if we look at a rotating disc on which a spiral has been painted, we feel dazed and dizzy. Or, waiting at a red traffic light, when the car in front of us rolls backwards, we automatically put our foot down on the brake instead of reversing — because it felt as if we were rolling forwards. And everyone is familiar with this: two trains stand parallel to each other on the platform. One is about to set off in one direction, the other in the opposite direction. We sit in one of the trains and look out at the windows of the other. And suddenly one of the trains is moving. But which one?

The human brain alters our perceptions in certain situations, placing actual reality into a sequence of other realities felt to be similarly genuine. This inbuilt brain function of disorientation is what the dyslexic activates, finding in it the capacity to resolve confusion and by this means to gain insight.

Rudolf Steiner describes this process in very similar terms:

When I see my own body, this body itself is already a deduction. The idea is only present inasmuch as I direct my eyes to the body; and as I now carry out a certain, semi-conscious or unconscious procedure, I bring things together in an evaluating sense, allowing a whole experience to arise, which one can summarize as 'This is a body.' [14]

One might even interpret Steiner's comments relating to the attainment of 'higher knowledge' — for instance lecture 2 in the 'Spiritual Ground' cycle (August 17, 1922, GA 305) and in *Occult Science* (GA 13) — as further descriptions of the disorientation function.

The dyslexic thus uses disorientation in order to perceive more than one reality and to acquire multi-layered perceptions. In this way he can make observations from various different perspectives and obtain more information than others do. At the same time this alters his actual sensory perceptions (apart from the senses of smell and taste): visual and auditory perception, the sense of touch, of balance and time.

Outside observers can easily see this, and all traditional (modern) therapy approaches for dyslexics — also in the anthroposophical domain — work hard to school the senses. Such approaches are often very arduous; in my view they are questionable since they aim to cure symptoms rather than enquiring into the causes: 'The big drawback here is that dyslexia isn't a disease, but a self-created condition.' [15]

Rudolf Steiner notes at the start of his lectures on curative education:

At least to a small degree we can discern in the great majority of people things such as losing your train of thought, or an inability to keep the right distance between spoken words so that you either trip over your tongue or the listener could almost go for a little walk between two words; or similar irregularities that can surface in the life of will and feeling ... In these matters one needs to study the symptoms, just as every physician speaks of symptoms in his case histories ... but will never confuse the complex of symptoms with the underlying content of the illness.

And he tries to cast light on these underlying causes for he too saw that genius may be hidden there:

Basically we have no right to speak of 'normality' or 'abnormality' in the mental and emotional life of a child, or in any human being, other than by examining what is the average 'normal' condition. There is no other criterion than the common denominator in a community of philistines ...

This is why judgements are so very confused when one begins to diagnose an abnormality and starts doing all sorts of things in the belief it is helping — instead of which one is banishing a small piece of genius. [16]

During a seminar Ronald Davis said: 'You don't need therapy to understand talent or genius, you only have to add something.'

A further characteristic of the dyslexic is 'non-verbal conceptualization' or in other words: 'Thinking with mental pictures of concepts or ideas; any form of thinking that does not use words. Intuition is a form of non-verbal conceptualization.' [17]

'Verbal conceptualization' stands counter to this: 'Thinking with the sounds of words. Hearing your thoughts in words is a form of verbal conceptualization'.[18] Since (potential) dyslexics automatically and unconsciously use the disorientation function of their brain in infancy to identify objects in their environment — and thus discover that this seems to work for them — they have no reason to develop analytic and logical thinking to consciously perceive objects.

In normal (i.e. non-dyslexic) childhood development, the skills for analytical reasoning and logic should begin to develop at around the age of three. These are the skills for consciously recognizing, and children who need these skills begin to develop them. But little P.D. (dyslexic child) already has a system that is faster and more accurate than analytical reasoning and logic could ever be. He has no need of those 'normal' skills at all, so they don't develop.

Children who need skills of analytical reasoning and logic must also start to develop their skills of verbal conceptualization, because reasoning and logic are language-based processes. These forms of thinking occur in the same patterns as sentences. So a normal child must use the speech and language centre on the left side of the brain in his or her thought processes.

This explains why verbal conceptualization is many times slower than non-verbal conceptualization: the speech and language centre of the brain must, of necessity, operate at the maximum intelligible speed of speech — at most perhaps 250 words per minute or four words per second. The result is that the normal child's thinking process is dramatically slowing down, while P.D.'s mind continues to race along at full speed.

P.D. has, of course, learned to understand spoken language and can talk. In fact, he sometimes tries to talk as fast as he can think, and his mouth can't keep up with his mind. When he is trying to say something he considers important, his speech speeds up so much that the words run together. What his parents hear is an unintelligible garble of sounds. They worry that he is developing a stutter.

'Slow down, darling,' says his mother. 'You're talking so fast I can't understand what you're saying.' To P.D., who is trying to describe a thought he is visualizing, her speech sounds agonisingly slow.

It's as if she is speaking at the rate of less than one ... word ... per ... second.

Estimates of the speed differential between verbal and non-verbal conceptualization range from 400 to 2,000 times faster when people use the non-verbal mode. The reality is probably somewhere in between.

The process of developing verbal conceptualization skills (thinking with the sounds of language) can take up to two years. Once it fully develops, it will become the primary mode of thinking of most children. So by the age of five, at about the time primary school begins, normal children have already begun to think with the sound of words. This may be slow, but it will come in handy when they begin learning to read. [19]

All literacy programmes in schools are rooted in the analytic and logical approach, and are thus based on verbal thinking:

Around the age of seven, the child is able to penetrate these pictorial/cognitive contents with consciously experienced and guided activity. He can engage with things through consciously experienced autonomous activity. He acquires the capacity to observe the objects of his perception with inwardly directed consciousness, e.g. in relation to their different parts and elements. This analytic mode of observation is necessary if the child is to hear the sound configuration of words in a way that allows the sequence of individual sounds to be consciously accentuated as elements of these words. [20]

What mode of thinking underlies the following statements by Rudolf Steiner? Is it an analytical and logical one?

But when I perceive a word, I do not live my way so intimately into the object, into the external entity, as when I perceive the thought through the word. Most people don't bother with such distinctions. But there is a difference between perceiving a mere word, a sound with meaning, and a real perception of the thought behind this word. [21]

While it is true that we can form all cognitive images into words such as 'tree,' very few people think exclusively in images:

For instance, you hear a word such as 'tree.' When you hear the word 'tree' then your etheric body quietly speaks the word 'tree' too — not your physical but your etheric body. [22]

Is Steiner simply referring here to an inwardly spoken repetition of the word? No:

What we have in the etheric body is pictorial work. Into the etheric body is incorporated what we can call symbolism ... The etheric body processes in symbolism, as in dream, what no longer resembles external impressions, and this is what the continuing resonance of the speech sound consists of. [23]

Below he describes in quite logical terms the development of the child in terms of first dreaming of the sensory world — and thus not sensorily oriented — through to understanding of speech via non-verbal thinking. He is not, therefore, referring to directed consciousness or analytic observation.

We therefore see the child's inner disposition as revealed in the threefold sequence of 'walking — speaking — thinking' as it were united and combined in the pictorial element.

In this second phase of life, between the change of teeth and puberty, what the child first absorbed in a dream of the sensory world as the actions of his environment is, remarkably, transformed into images. One can say that the child starts to dream of what his surroundings do, whereas in the first phase of life he grasped it very neutrally, neutrally in his own particular way, by inwardly imitating it.

Now he begins to dream of what his surroundings do. And the child's thoughts, his life of thinking, are not yet abstract, not yet logical thoughts, but are still pictures.

The child lives, between the change of teeth and puberty, in an element where speech is decisive — in this artistic, aesthetic, pictorial element. From us adults the only thing that penetrates to him is what is immersed in this pictorial element.[24]

It is clear therefore that we have a conflict: whoever uses the two dyslexic capacities of 'disorientation' and 'non-verbal concept formation' is likely to have problems in learning the cultural techniques of reading and writing, at least as taught by traditional educational methods.

From Natural Talent to Disability

The dyslexic child thus uses his special talent for perception, the gift of disorientation, and his pictorial thinking, to resolve confusion — or in other words to understand what is unknown. He usually succeeds very well at this as an infant, because he is, of course, primarily concerned with actual physical objects.

Based on this experience he will now unconsciously not only disorientate himself when he encounters an unknown but graspable object, but also when he meets a confusing, abstract symbol which cannot be grasped in three dimensions, e.g. lines and strokes supposed to produce letters or combinations of letters, which also have no pictorial relation. And here, suddenly, his wonderful mechanism for understanding and recognition no longer functions.

What happens when the child activates his multi-level perceptive function in the disorientation mode? He automatically sees the symbol, the letter or the word, from various directions and angles: forwards, backwards, standing on its head in both directions and floating in space. The picture 'tree' always remains a tree from all angles. But an *i* from above? And a *b* backwards? The confusion is not resolved, but instead it grows.

Ronald Davis writes of this:

To see the effect of non-verbal thinking on little P.D., let's make him five years old and send him to primary school. No matter how prepared he was for this day, and no matter how enthusiastically he was looking forward to it, the reality is terrifying.

He is in a strange place. There he sits. He's scared to death. He would rather be anywhere else in the world than where he is.

Now let's have a strange lady go up to the blackboard with a piece of chalk and write the letters C-A-T. She turns round and says, 'Who knows what this is?' Some of the other kids have already learned the word, but P.D. doesn't know. Even when they say 'cat', he makes no connection. The lines don't form anything like his mental picture of a cat. [25]

Rudolf Steiner describes this situation in precisely the same way:

And when the child enters school we find that he has most opposition to reading and writing. For you see, here is a man: he has black or blonde hair, a forehead, nose, eyes; he has legs and walks, takes hold of things, says something and has certain thoughts — and this is his father. But now the child is supposed to see the symbol — FATHER — as his father. There is no reason why he should, not the slightest reason ... [26]

In this context, Rudolf Steiner's own first experiences of school are noteworthy:

My father was keen for me to learn to read and write at an early age. When I reached school age I was sent to the village school. The teacher was an old gentleman, who found teaching a burdensome occupation. I never believed for a moment that I could learn anything from him.

After an unfortunate incident (he was wrongly accused of a misdemeanour), his father removed him from school:

And now my father took over teaching me himself. I sat for hours beside him in his office, and was supposed to write and read while he did his administrative work in between. With him too I couldn't form any real interest in what I was supposed to absorb as lessons ...

When I wrote I did it because I had to; in fact I did it as fast as possible to fill a page speedily. After that I could take blotting sand and scatter it on what I had written, and was fascinated to see how quickly the sand absorbed the ink, and the extent to which it swelled up with the ink. I repeatedly felt the letters with my fingers ... and this is how I ... approached the letters. [27]

This 'childish playing' by the young Rudolf Steiner, which gave his '... attempts at writing a form that did not in the least please my father ...' are not something that should just be dismissed with a smile. Still less, however, should one diagnose them — along with the rest of the behaviour he describes — as 'concentration problem,' 'school refusal' or 'learning difficulty.'

What the little 'bumbler' was doing there, in focusing on 'physical properties' was grasping the ungraspable, and giving the abstract a form and image. The letters covered in blotting sand had assumed form, and could thus be felt and experienced from all sides.

'And despite everything, I learned to read well at a relatively early age.'

A contradiction?

No, for here he relates how he read a book on geometry. When a two-dimensional symbol always gave the same meaning even when viewed in many different ways by the circling mind's eye, this gave him a feeling of happiness. A triangle, a rectangle or a circle always retain their characteristics even when seen from left or right, from above or below.

I threw myself into this with enthusiasm. For weeks my soul was entirely filled with congruence or similarity between triangles, rectangles, polygons. I racked my head to work out where parallels actually intersect; the Pythagorean theorem entranced me ... I know that I first found happiness through geometry.

I wanted to be able to tell myself that experience of the mental world is just as little an illusion as the sensory world. In geometry, I told myself, was a knowledge only the soul experiences through its own powers. And in this feeling I found a justification for speaking of the world of mind or spirit which I experienced, as much as of the sensory world. And so I spoke of it. I had two images which, though they were vague, still played an important part in my life before I was eight years old. I differentiated things and beings which 'one sees' from those which 'one doesn't see.' [28]

It is indisputable that Rudolf Steiner subsequently succeeded, somehow, in learning to read and write, yet doing so 'maltreated' him. He managed to read, I suspect, by teaching himself and, driven by his great thirst for knowledge, perhaps also by guessing. With writing he strove for phonetic spelling by imagining sounds he had heard others speaking — that is, by forming 'sound pictures' for himself.

As a boy I would read 'past' the words, focusing my soul directly on views, concepts and ideas so that reading gave me nothing at all in the way of developing a sense for correct spelling and grammar.

When writing, on the other hand, I felt the urge to fix the word images in sounds in the way I mostly heard them as dialect words. This meant that I had enormous difficulties in finding my way into writing correctly. [29]

A dyslexic once told me how he noted or recalled names, through the 'image of the sound': 'I see the person in front of me but then often can't remember his name. Then I imagine another person who is addressing him, and then the name comes back to me.'

But we should not overlook the fact here that Rudolf Steiner mentions in several other places that he could 'read well' in his childhood and youth, although correct spelling and grammar did not come easily to him. There are in fact dyslexics who learn to read early — usually teaching themselves — but are unable to use the word images they read when it comes to writing.

Behind this 'good reading' however might lie an understanding of the books acquired through the immediate perception he describes, for Steiner always mentions his reading ability in connection with pictorial representations such as, initially, books on geometry. Later, when he was eleven, this led to books on mathematics and physics. And he adds: 'I kept repeating my efforts to read; and each time it got easier.'

And a long time before the geometry book, Rudolf Steiner had in fact embarked on his first 'reading experiences' as follows:

Among my toys I was particularly drawn to the kind which I still consider especially good today. These were picture books with moveable figures that you could pull from beneath on strings. With these pictures you could follow little stories, which you helped bring to life yourself by pulling on the strings. I often spent hours in front of these picture books with my sister. Through them, as if naturally, I learned the bases of reading. [30]

And what are dyslexic children particularly fascinated by today?

The value of some of the more 'trashy' picture books and comics is debatable, but you'll find children wholly absorbed in 'reading' them — as they themselves like to recall the way they turn the pages with dizzy speed.

And while we may get inwardly or outwardly agitated about such 'trash' we overlook the fact (since we are not word-blind, but no doubt picture-blind) that the genius of the non-verbal thinker has, before our eyes, devoured the whole comic in minutes. The speed of it is really such that the 'reader' will be on to the third page in the time it takes us to read two speech bubbles.

Let's just reflect for a moment on all that Rudolf Steiner accomplished: his studies, doctorate, his whole life's work. How did he do it? I suspect (after reading his pedagogical suggestions) that he did so through a combination of his gift for self-teaching, his knowledge and insight, and the teaching methods common at that time. Examining this further does not belong here but to another chapter (see Parts II and III). The main thing is that Rudolf Steiner succeeded in working his way through the world of letters. But what he did not do is feel at home with them, let alone love them. Throughout his life, he continued to regard letters as 'little demons' whose use should be postponed for as long as possible:

When the Europeans arrived in America ... the Indians took to their heels because they thought the letters shown to them were little devils; and they said: 'The palefaces ... communicate through little devils or demons.'

But that's exactly what letters are too for children. They mean nothing to them. The child feels — and he's right — that there's something demonic in letters. Because they are signs and symbols they can be used magically. One has to start from a picture instead. The picture is not a magic symbol but something real, and it is out of this element we need to work.

But people come along and say: 'Yes, but children will be late in learning to read and write if you do this.' They only say this because they do not know how harmful it is if children learn to read and write at a young age. It is very bad if one can write when young. The kind of reading and writing we have today is really only suited for a later age, around eleven or twelve.

And the more one is blessed by being unable to read and write well early on, the better this will be later in life. Someone who cannot yet write properly at the age of fourteen or fifteen — I'm speaking from my own experience: I couldn't when I was fourteen and fifteen — does not place as many obstacles in the way of his spiritual development as someone who can write and read perfectly at the age of seven and eight.

These are things the teacher, in particular, must really observe. [31]

Native American hieroglyphics story. The spiral of the story runs from the centre to the periphery.

Victory

In his own research on himself, Ronald Davis discovered:

> *The dyslexic person needs to learn how to turn the disorientation switch on and off. This is accomplished by consciously positioning the mind's eye. When it is moved to a certain place, the person stops being disorientated and is able to perceive the outside or 'real' world correctly. The person becomes orientated.* [32]

Dyslexics distort written script particularly when it's connected with activities in which their 'talent' is working at full throttle. In Ronald Davis's case, his writing became particularly indecipherable when he was modelling and wanted to write something down at the same time. He therefore concluded that the underlying structure (brain or nervous system) was not really disordered but that the problem must be triggered by a different factor. He thus discovered his 'orientation point' (which he also calls the 'comfort zone', accompanied by a feeling of well-being), from where he no longer perceived the 'real' world in a distorted way, but correctly: 'A stable location above and behind the head (this location varies from person to person). Put your mind's eye on the orientation point.' [33]

Rudolf Steiner was also aware of this, and there is a corresponding drawing by him.[34] He believed that this point lies in the centre of the 'etheric heart,' located outside of the body, which establishes a connection with knowledge.

In retrospect, therefore, one can also explain why Rudolf Steiner's spelling became so noticeably irregular during his lectures on curative education. To diagnose the cases he was presenting he placed himself — whether consciously or unconsciously — into the state of disorientation, which enabled him, through one of his special gifts, to make such brilliant observations: 'reading human beings' as Ronald Davis puts it.

This talent (the perceptive capacity of disorientation) can be a very significant advantage which improves abilities in the following domains: spatial awareness, reading human beings, strategic planning, technical arts, drama/role play, music/dancing, driving vehicles, technology/engineering, telling stories. [35]

By consciously switching the disorientation function of his brain on and off, the dyslexic can learn to master his perception. He can control it. (Ronald Davis describes in detail how such orientation training is undertaken in his book *The Gift of Dyslexia*).

But this is just a first step. Using orientation so that one no longer sees a letter or word flying all over the place — from below and above, from right and left — is just the basic condition whereby the mind's eye and the physical eye can calmly grasp the symbol in its two-dimensional form. The second step is to master its sense as well.

Training of symbol mastery must therefore be founded on orientation training, first and foremost in learning the entire alphabet. Every letter is made 'graspable' by means of modelling the alphabet first in capitals and then small letters in plasticine, and repeatedly checking its orientation. In this way the dyslexic quickly learns to un-demonize the text symbols and to control them.

Left: From the German edition of The Gift of Dyslexia, © *Ariston Verlag*
Right: Rudolf Steiner's drawing of 'the orientation point'.

To lead this on to establishing or improving the dyslexic's ability to read, Ronald Davis then developed a method called 'Spell-Reading,' which — and this can happen even for a non-reader in a matter of minutes — passes over into a whole-word method and then, in a third stage, achieves a pictorial absorption of content. I initially thought this was unbelievable, but it really is a *spelling* and not *phonetic* method.

Once again, the parallel with Steiner is astonishing. He writes:

The normal method using [whole] words only reaches the physical body. The phonetic method already approaches the soul level and, as horrible as it is to say so, the spelling method takes one right into the domain of soul. The latter is still an idiocy today, but it is nevertheless more soulful; but it can't be directly applied. [36]

Gerrit, aged 16

In Spell-Reading (as in every other kind of reading) one inevitably encounters words that bear no pictorial element in them, or words the reader (as yet) has no experience of, and therefore cannot picture. Such words can be abstract terms of any kind, but primarily they are the most commonly used words such as prepositions, conjunctions, pronouns and articles. Ronald Davis calls them 'trigger words.'

When a trigger word appears, the dyslexic immediately switches on the disorientation switch; and confusion, with all the accompanying phenomena we have described, overwhelms him.

All these words were already part of the speech vocabulary of each one of these people by the time they were five. What was lacking was an image or concept for the meaning of each word. Because the dyslexic mainly thinks in images, they were unable to think with words for which they had no concepts or images. [37]

For Rudolf Steiner, too, it was important to eventually 'decipher' such words. In this context he quotes Jean Paul as follows:

Trust in time's decoding function, and that of the context. A child of five understands the words 'of course,' 'maybe,' 'however,' 'surely,' but just try giving an explanation of their meaning — not to the child but to his father! A whole philosopher is hiding in that little word 'although.' [38]

To master the trigger words, the 'blank images' as Davis also calls them, the symbol mastery method that was used in learning the alphabet is employed. The dyslexic makes a three-dimensional picture of the word by representing its meaning and the 'text picture' as a model in plasticine. Ronald Davis also recommends this symbol mastery technique for teachers of dyslexics, so they can learn to grasp concepts better.

On August 18, 1924, Rudolf Steiner likewise recommended the following for pupils and teachers:

This is why the child certainly has an urge to model forms ... if, as teacher, you know what the child likes modelling ... you will be able to offer him helpful guidance ...

Therefore, since today's teacher training courses as yet do nothing of the kind, it is important for the teacher himself to try his hand at modelling. You will find that however much you may have learned about a liver or, let us say, some complex interrelationship of blood vessels, you still won't be able to model it in wax or plasticine. Suddenly you will find that you develop a quite different insight ...

Now it's very interesting that if you simply let children get on with it, after describing some aspect of the human being — the lung or another organ — they will start creating forms that are very similar to the lung or suchlike, quite by themselves ...

And that's why it's necessary to really engage with this sculptural approach, to find a way to ... really copy the forms, with wax or plasticine or — why not, our children often do it — with dirt from the road. Well, if you don't have anything else, that will do fine.

This is the inner urge, the etheric body's inner yearning, to model and paint like this. That's why it's so easy to draw on this yearning and derive the letters from the forms which the child paints, or from the forms he models. If you do this you are really teaching out of an insight into human nature. This must happen at every level. It is very interesting to see how the child models out of his own innate nature. [39]

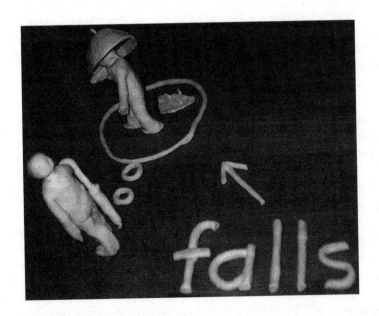

Plasticine model for 'in case' (reprinted by kind permission of the German Davis Dyslexia Association)

Taking Stock

Ronald Davis discovered methods for effectively overcoming dyslexia. Since 1982, working with a team of scientists from various disciplines, he has researched and developed his findings at the Reading Research Council and the Dyslexia Correction Center, which he founded in California. He has found that:
- Orientation corrects perception
- Mastery of symbols corrects dyslexia

When words that previously had no image attached to them are filled pictorially, the dyslexic no longer needs to use his special perception capacity of disorientation. He remains orientated in relation to text and its symbols, and he learns to think pictorially with words. Dyslexia gradually fades; but the talent or gift remains: the 'gift of mastery.'

When someone masters something, it becomes a part of that person. It becomes part of the individual's thought and creative process. It adds the quality of its essence to all subsequent thought and creativity of the individual. [40]

However, learning to control trigger words and abstract terms by the method of symbol mastery may not only improve reading ability and language understanding in dyslexics but in everyone else too.

For some years now, at various 'entirely normal' primary schools in California, a trial has been underway using Ronald Davis's methods. Its original aim was as a preventive programme to avoid dyslexia developing; but the results show that schooling of pictorial thinking not only prevented dyslexia but also nurtured a range of quite other, unexpected abilities, such as better language understanding and creative skills in elaborate thinking.

The precise findings have now been published (www.dyslexia.com), and a start has been made on offering special teacher training courses geared to this.

Alongside these current discoveries, I'd like to cite Rudolf Steiner again:

We live in the fifth post-Atlantean epoch, which will be succeeded by the sixth and then the seventh. Hitherto ... as people on earth, we have developed a certain tendency to abstract thinking, to non-pictorial thinking. But before this fifth post-Atlantean era comes to an end, pictorial thinking, imagination must develop. The special task of this fifth post-Atlantean epoch is in fact to develop the gift of imagination in human beings on earth. [41]

I'd like to add an example here from my own experience with dyslexic children and adolescents, to give a sense of the kinds of comment pictorial thinking facilitates:

'I know where the end of the world is.'
'Yes, where is it?'
'Behind my back!'
(girl, age 11)

In daily interaction with dyslexic children and adolescents, I am always learning more. Their fascinating, lightning-quick pictorial thinking keeps opening up new perspectives for me, which I often only later recognize. I am convinced that we can all learn an endless amount from them.

Of course not every dyslexic is or will become a Leonardo or an Einstein, but we will only really see and acknowledge their gifts if our schools offer them non-verbal techniques, so that they learn the indispensable 'cultural techniques' of reading and writing. At the same time, children who primarily think verbally will also find expanded opportunities for learning, as the pilot programme is already demonstrating in California. I hope so — for Waldorf schools especially.

The cover of F. Carlgren's book *Erziehung zur Freiheit* (Education for Freedom) carries the following quote from Steiner:

We should not ask what people need to know and to be able to do for the already existing social order; but instead we should ask what inherent disposition exists in people and what can be developed from this.

Then it will be possible for the social order to benefit from the ever-replenished forces streaming towards it from the younger generation.

Then this social order will also always embody what the full potential of human beings makes of it; and then the younger generation will not be moulded into what the existing social order tries to make of them.

In an interview with Saskia Seltzer (in *Ab 40*), Ronald Davis expresses the same idea:

In my view, these gifts are being wasted everywhere in the world due to our education system. How long can we afford to go on doing this? We need these gifts to assure our society continues.

But even if we believe we have recognized Rudolf Steiner's approach and way of thinking, really understanding his brilliant ideas remains a challenge:

I will never speak about any spiritual matter that I am not fully familiar with from my own, most immediate spiritual experience. That is my guiding star. And it has helped me avoid all pitfalls and illusions.

I can see through the illusions. And I believe I can say that the spiritual is as entirely real as the table on which I write these words.

Someone who desired to understand everything about me would find harmony where — since he does not understand me — he sees only contradiction.[42]

It is also worth remembering that quite a few have 'fought the battle' with letters:

I just want to point out that many have forgotten that [he] was never able to spell properly; that in fact he made mistakes throughout his life, especially when young.[43]

So he left the proper spelling of his literary works to a professional amanuensis, since this caused him 'senseless torment' and was 'an overwhelming annoyance.'[44]

Who are they referring to, you ask? None other than the author of *Faust* ...

Part II

... But let's focus on the area of real capabilities

The Gift of Dyslexia

Some time has have passed (the original German edition of this book was published in 2000) since my booklet 'How we have been maltreated ...' was published. And this time has been packed with interesting conversations and encounters, but also further and deeper questions that still await an answer.

Since those September days of 1997, my work with dyslexic children and adolescents has continually increased in scope, intensity and not least success. I have developed lively dialogues with people affected by dyslexia, from the most varied social and age groups, who describe to me their astonishment at feeling suddenly 'understood.'

I will now add some important aspects to what has been said so far; I'd like to begin where I ended before.

Rudolf Steiner once again

In a letter of 1903, he too described his sense of not being understood:

I have been much misunderstood; and will doubtless go on being so. This lies in the nature of my path. I have been regarded as all sorts of things, not least a fanatic of one type or another. If there's one thing I know I'm not, it's a fanatic, for fanaticism really seduces one into illusion; and I have always stood by the principle of avoiding all illusion.

You write that I embody the spirit in my life. In <u>one</u> respect, I assure you, I certainly strive to do so: I will never speak about any <u>spiritual</u> matter that I am not fully familiar with from my own, most immediate spiritual <u>experience</u>. That is my guiding star. And it has helped me avoid all pitfalls and illusions ...

And I believe I can say that the spiritual is as entirely real as the table on which I write these words. Someone who desired to understand <u>everything</u> about me would find harmony where — since he does not understand me — he sees only contradiction.

But Steiner's letter was of course not written in line with new German spelling rules: in the original German text there is a comma too many, a full stop is missing, and instead of 'In one respect' (*'In einer Hinsicht'*) he has written 'I one respect' (*'Ich einer Hinsicht'*).

One of the contradictions one finds when reflecting on Rudolf Steiner and his life and work is that this highly qualified mind clearly struggled with letters. In Part I, I described how appalled his teacher was at the eight-year-old's writing, for: 'I rounded all my letters, ignored the ascenders and misspelled all words.'

It is hard to credit this admission today when one examines his fine copperplate script. But he frequently states how much he suffered as a child when learning to write — formulated either more biographically as in his *Autobiography*, or more philosophically, as in *Occult Science*. There he writes:

For the I or ego, memory and forgetting closely resemble what waking and sleeping are for the astral body. Just as sleep allows the cares and anxieties of the day to fade away into nothing, so forgetting spreads a veil over life's unhappy experiences, and thus extinguishes some of the past.

And just as sleep is necessary for exhausted life forces to be renewed and strengthened, so we must banish certain parts of our past from memory if we are to be free and open towards new experiences. It is precisely from forgetting that we derive strength for perceiving the new.

Think of something like learning to write. All the little details the child has to experience and undergo in learning to write are forgotten. What remains is the ability to write.

How would we ever manage to write if, each time we put pen to paper, all the experiences we underwent when learning to write were to surface again as memory? [45]

Did Rudolf Steiner simply forget 'life's unhappy experiences' and everything he 'underwent when learning to write?' How did he win the battle with letters, without allowing himself to be further 'maltreated?' Here lies the mystery. For me, Rudolf Steiner is the proof that there are ways to overcome literacy problems by drawing on very specific structures of thinking innate to the human being.

My concern here is to recognize and understand these structures and to use them to address problems of literacy — and not in the least to prove whether, or how much, or for how long Rudolf Steiner was a dyslexic. The example of Rudolf Steiner is used here solely in an attempt to trace the special mode of thinking underlying the phenomenon of dyslexia.

In my view, Rudolf Steiner's statements on education conceal many suggestions for how to avoid dyslexia ever developing as a 'disorder.' Rather than sacrificing the thinking underlying dyslexia, however, this approach can preserve and nurture it.

For Steiner as for Davis, literacy problems do not reveal a 'deficit' or 'deficiency' but instead a particular gift, an added plus. And both of them have been and continue to be widely misunderstood — or at least stand in flagrant opposition to prevailing views and school practice — even sometimes the practice at Steiner-Waldorf schools.

The lack of any prospect that his views on education would make an impression on school policy regulators led Steiner to ideas that come close to 'conspiratorial.' In the book that compiles his meetings with teachers at the Stuttgart Waldorf school, he said:

And so articles would need to be published — of course without it being apparent that it originates from our address ... The school inspectors ought to play a part here. Articles would be needed from the most varied points of view showing that it really is very important for a child if he learns to read properly between the age of eight and nine. Examples could be cited, such as that Goethe could not read and write before the age of nine, and that Helmholtz only learned to read and write at a much later age. Then, on the other hand, one could show that there are also people who were able to read and write at the age of four or five but who later became buffoons. [46]

In other words, Steiner regards early reading and writing as harmful, and based on his own experience would prefer children to begin with it somewhere between the ages of eleven and fifteen. He even states that he would 'congratulate' the parents of a child who could not yet read or write at the age of nine. [47]

But this view of his met with no response, either then or now.

Traditional ideas about the causes

In general, children of only seven or eight who have not yet developed literacy skills are diagnosed as having the 'partial' disorder of dyslexia or literacy impairment — or whatever term happens to be in current use. Tests at pre-school age try to diagnose this still earlier.

Once an 'official' diagnosis has been made, most regions of Germany allow opting out of literacy 'skills grading,' although a very long-winded procedure is required for this, involving expert reports and so forth; this in turn triggers years of special support for the child.

Even the diagnostic process is an enormous burden for a child:

For a complete, supposedly 'certain' diagnosis, the child is required to visit the GP, a paediatrician, an optician, an ear, nose and throat specialist and sometimes even a neurologist.

If all tests and examinations prove negative — which happens relatively frequently — the children concerned are, as experience shows, referred elsewhere and shipped around (usually to university clinics) until some kind of 'anomaly' is eventually ascertained.

This process is not by any means due to bad will or medical profiteering, but simply reflects the helplessness of professionals. [48]

Around 60 different causes of dyslexia are currently being considered. These range from developmental and brain maturation delays (caused, for example, by laterality problems, perception problems, anatomical damage and metabolic problems) through to psychological and social factors and to 'brain damage.' In the field of molecular genetics, even genes are now being considered, supported by the observation that several children in some families are dyslexic, and that this therefore seems to be a dominant inherited trait.

There is rare interdisciplinary harmony amongst psychologists, doctors, educationalists, teachers, speech therapists, movement therapists and other experts in their search for the cause of this 'disorder.'

From an anthroposophical perspective, too, failure to get to grips with reading and writing is currently assumed to indicate a learning or developmental 'disorder.' Even at age eight/nine (Class Three), a 'developmental delay' is diagnosed in such cases. In Dutch Steiner schools, a 'Class Two' test (age seven/eight) has been introduced. [49]

And Rosemarie Jänchen concludes:

Whoever does not learn to read and write in their first two years of schooling will need two to three years to do so as an adult. This shows that these techniques very much belong to the stage of childhood which we generally characterize as school readiness. [50]

There are occasional references in anthroposophical literature to famous dyslexics such as Paul Ehrlich, and even observations relating to 'special gifts' and 'valuable qualities' in dyslexic children. For example, Monik Terlouw writes at the end of her book on dyslexia:

Being dyslexic does not just mean that there are all sorts of things one cannot do, but also that one has gifts in certain areas: vivid, pictorial thinking, good visual-spatial memory and the ability to be able to 'think well with your hands' are valuable qualities that are welcome in many professions. [51]

Nevertheless, here too the assumption is of a basic 'deficiency' which should be treated and remedied as early as possible.

The opposite stance: dyslexia as a gift

My own experience and observations, on the other hand, have persuaded me that the one thing that ought to happen early on with potential dyslexics is to recognize the phenomenon and not remedy it. Early recognition must, on the contrary, give rise to targeted support of the determinants of dyslexia rather than combating them. Why do I say this?

If dyslexia is really rooted in a gift, as Ronald Davis found in himself and showed convincingly in his book, the gift should not be therapied away, but must instead be used by taking advantage of the strength innate in it to master the secondary symptoms.

In his works, Rudolf Steiner did not specifically speak about 'dyslexia' and its treatment, but nevertheless I cite him as my chief witness. Referring to the problems which Johann Wolfgang Goethe had throughout his life with spelling and grammar, Steiner once remarked:

> ... I believe I am particularly qualified to speak about this, for reasons which you may be able to detect between the lines of what I am saying ... Instead of always regretting that [children] cannot spell properly, and continually asking 'What shall we do so that they learn to spell,' it would be much better to reflect on where their true abilities lie, if not in this sphere — and to find this sphere of their real gifts, and build a bridge to it in some way, so that such people can if necessary also learn and absorb what they must. [52]

The reason that this and many other similar remarks by Steiner have received so little attention may be because they were not considered in relation to the debate about dyslexia. If, however, one relates Steiner's comments to Moniek Terlouw's observations above, we can start to see why the Davis method in particular is such a promising way of mastering dyslexia.

But if the sphere where the real gifts lie is not sought, let alone found, a young dyslexic, with all his gifts, will face the dilemma of varying expectations: parents get agitated when their child does not develop literacy skills at the 'right time' (when society expects it); the teacher may urge patience and comfort them, saying the skills will develop; the therapist on the other hand may be at pains to bring the little 'dreamer' as fast as possible down from whichever heaven he's in (perhaps the realm where those 'true gifts' lie), and so on. The child, equipped with that dyslexic ability to 'read' people, tries to please everyone, and his self-esteem takes a battering.

I absolutely do not wish to criticize parents, teachers or therapists, and certainly not specialist authors, in their search for ways to remedy dyslexia. But I would like to encourage them, or at least awaken their curiosity, to consider Ronald Davis's findings in their ongoing efforts. My own experience, at least, is that after reading Davis one sees everything in a new light. If, for instance, I had always known of Davis's insight into 'pictorial (non-verbal) thinking' which, along with the disorientation gift, underlies dyslexia as a causal factor, I might have been able to recognize things that have taken me long and gradual steps to acknowledge. For example, I would then have been able to connect the problems of dyslexia that were already occupying me with the research conducted by P. Rozin and his colleagues in 1971 — which I knew about — relating to the experiences of dyslexic children with non-alphabetic script systems:

> *In this connection, three American psychologists at Pennsylvania University have run an interesting trial on reading impairment (dyslexia) in children. Such children have difficulty in composing words and sentences from single letters — both when writing and reading.*
>
> *After many attempts, the three researchers succeeded in finding the right point of entry with an interesting trick, quickly enabling the children to read whole sentences more or less without mistakes.*
>
> *Astonishingly, it was observed that these children were much better able to deal with Chinese pictograms, with brush-drawn word symbols, than with our European alphabet. After only five or ten minutes they could read simple sentences in such a character script.*
>
> *And after about four hours, much quicker than other children, they were able to understand a whole story, whereas before they could scarcely read a word, let alone a longer sentence, even after days of practice.* [53]

In his essay 'A graduated model for the development of children's reading and writing strategies,' Klaus B. Günther also speaks of early trials with non-alphabetic script systems:

> *In non-alphabetic script systems such as the Chinese Hanzi and Japanese Kanji, whose primary units represent morphemes or words (Coulmas, 1983), Kwee Young and Yuko Kimura (quoted in Bryant/Bradley 1983, p 173/176) have shown that, corresponding with the character of these script systems, a much more developed logographemic strategy predominates; and this, according to Makita (1968) means that only 1% of school children show any reading difficulties.* [54]

Surely this research could have told me that problems in literacy might be connected with our alphabetic script, and that their cause could therefore be sought in the system itself and the way it is taught rather than in the individual child and his 'developmental disorder' or 'brain damage.'

Without knowing or wanting this, I believe I was simply too stuck in my received ideas of dyslexia as 'deficiency,' 'disorder,' 'illness' or 'wrongness.'

Since reading Davis, I have thrown these traditional explanations and evaluation models out of the window. I'm sure that public opinion on dyslexia and thus the position of dyslexics within society will change a great deal in the future too.

Hearing from prominent dyslexics

In America, a series of more or less prominent people have started 'coming out' as dyslexics. If this spreads to Europe it will be interesting to see who they will be: who will no longer feel ashamed (if they ever did) but instead acknowledge their dyslexia openly, maybe even with pride.

For instance, the famous Danish architect Jørn Utzon, who designed the Sydney Opera House among other things, acknowledged what he still calls his own 'deficiency' in the journal *Living Architecture*:

I didn't become an engineer because I am both dyslexic and lack mathematical insight. One must have a mathematician's clear brain, which I admire, if one is to be a good engineer. Remember, geometry is something else. In compensation for these great deficiencies, my subnormalities, I have a strange, innate sense of space. I dream a house and then I have it in my head. This was something I could use as an architect. [55]

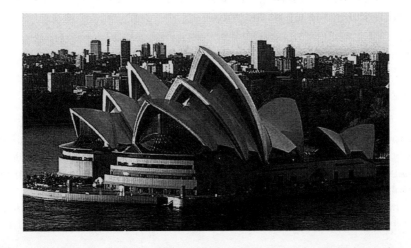

Also striking is an interview with the important mime artist, director, author and university professor Samy Molcho, which was published in a German Sunday newspaper under the title 'Everything's fine with me':

No one was supposed to find out that I can't write. If you live a hidden life you become inventive. I had to do well so that I could afford to get someone else to write my letters ...

Naturally I didn't write my six books myself, but I dictated them ... I don't understand words in a linear fashion, one after the other, but instead I see the whole picture, the totality ... In my view you've all been locked up in the one dimensionality of language. The word 'concept' is derived from a Latin term that means take hold of or grasp. Schools have forgotten this. Instead of working with things you can actually grasp hold of, they work with words ...

He laughs as he replies to whether a dyslexic has 'something wrong' in his brain:

Not at all. Everything's fine with me. It's just the measuring instruments that are wrong. Thinking three-dimensionally means having a different view of things and the world, and their potential ...

Of course not every dyslexic will be Leonardo, Einstein or Samy Molcho, but I have just heard about a case here in Hamburg where a boss was expressly looking for a dyslexic because he needed someone with 'multi-layered, far-sighted, "chaotic" thinking.' Maybe there will soon be more bosses like this around.

But how and when will assessment of dyslexics by those who dictate school policies change from 'disabled' to 'gifted' and start to inform our schooling system? It is still in the lap of the gods.

Spelling — an outmoded relic?

In Germany at the beginning of the eighties a start was actually made on 'officially' abolishing literacy impairment. Dyslexia was then seen as an artificially contrived term, since there would always inevitably be children who have problems learning to read and write.

Recently, however, at regional level, 'dyslexia rulings' have been issued once again, with specific diagnosis and support recommendations primarily to help prevent the spread of adult illiteracy in Germany. The nation is also clamouring about young people no longer being able to spell properly in the 'land of poets and thinkers' and is demanding greater efforts in schools to remedy this evil. The dwindling ability to spell is indeed an undeniable reality in Germany, and was proven to be so in 1995 by the Heidelberg psychologists Claudia Zerahn-Hartung and Ute Pfüller. The research does not show, however, that this state of affairs is an 'evil.' Nor does it show the opposite; and so everyone has to make their own assessment of the findings.

I, at least, would plead for people not to be over-hasty in joining the chorus of 'evil'-sayers.

On April 10, 1998, the *Stuttgarter Zeitung* reported on this research, which was awarded the Georg Siber prize. The study was based on 592 test subjects with German as their mother tongue. They ranged across all levels of education and professions, and were aged between sixteen and thirty:

The study was based on a standardized 'gap dictation' exercise (Althoff test: 'Mosel trip') for which, in 1968, only five per cent of young adults tested received the 'fail' mark. Today (1995), according to the two researchers, half of those tested were evaluated as 'not satisfactory' ...

The study is the first to offer statistical proof for the empirically supported suspicion that spelling and literacy skills have drastically deteriorated in recent decades ... Within a single generation, spelling errors have risen from ten to twenty, with men's performance in the dictation showing five more errors than that of women — a significant difference between the sexes.

The two psychologists believe that the drifting apart of ever poorer spelling and ever greater intellectual achievements points to a tendency for us to become a 'society of dyslexics.'

Whether Germany, with its half-baked spelling reform — officially introduced on August 1, 1998 — can counter this scenario in the longterm, is certainly dubious. But non-dyslexics — at least while they adjust to the new rules — may be a little more circumspect in the way they pass judgment on 'right' and 'wrong' in the spelling department.

Let me ask once more, heretically, what purpose is served by the graduation of 'perfect spellers' from schools? What stone-age technology is being honoured here as the West's greatest cultural asset, to the extent that it is used to distinguish between right and wrong, good and bad, above and below, and employment or unemployment?

Let's just look ahead to future technical developments for a moment: not prophetic vision, but entirely realistic:

In a few years, the computer keyboard I'm working on right now will be a prehistoric museum piece. We'll be speaking our texts into a microphone. The computer will write it all down for us — and its software will long since have decided whether to write 'dolphin' or 'dolfin.'

Anyone who wishes can already try out this future today. On August 28, 1998, the newspaper *Frankfurter Rundschau* ran the following story under the heading 'News from CeBIT':

Without keyboard or mouse
IBM is aiming to use better speech recognition technology to free computer users from mouse and keyboard. Using the program ViaVoice 98, dictation and commands can be inputted by voice. So far 128,000 words can be recognized, twice as many as previously.

You may be horrified at the thought, but Gottlieb Daimler's first car was prohibited in 1882 because of its terrifying speed of around twelve kilometres an hour, which frightened the horses. Of course that didn't stop it.

As in so many other things, it will not be possible to stop this 'progress' even if not everyone sees it as such. The nostalgic delight of riding in a horse-drawn coach when you're off to your wedding or on holiday will be matched, in a hundred years, by the idea of writing something down with a fountain pen in perfect spelling. But doing so will not make one into a more socially esteemed contemporary than the person who lets the computer do his writing for him.

As to a 'realistic' versus a 'prophetic' view of the future, Rudolf Steiner did not see any contradiction between them. In line with his nature and his knowledge of the world, a prophetic view was for him at the same time a realistic one. Thus, as long ago as October 14, 1913, in a lecture in Copenhagen, he foresaw the technological developments referred to above, assessed them and linked them to the human being's continuing soul-spiritual evolution:

Today people still learn to write. In a not too distant future people will only vaguely recall that we used to write in former centuries. There will be a kind of mechanized stenography which will be written on machines ...

Samples of handwriting will be dug up like Egyptian artefacts ... and just as the future will regard our handwritten documents in astonishment as something like Egyptian hieroglyphs, so at the same time human souls will be striving to receive the spirit's direct revelations once again. External life will become ever more externalized, but inner life will demand its rights ...

These are the two aspects of the future: on the one hand there will be ever-increasing desolation due to the superficiality of soul forces, but on the other, as a reaction against this desolation, soul forces in the depths will be invoked. To spread recognition of this we disseminate anthroposophy ...

Have no illusions about the future. But we do not give way to illusion about the future when we picture to ourselves how things will look in external, material life, and start from an observation such as that in future people will speak of handwriting as we speak of Egyptian hieroglyphs today ...

People in the future will speak of much that we still invest with soul qualities as of something long past ... Human beings will necessarily exchange the spirit of what is merely thought for that of direct vision ... [56]

Whatever the appearance and function of the future 'mechanized stenography' machine which is to relieve people of writing, it will (even if connected with human 'desolation') be nothing other than an externalization of outward life, which creates space for inner life to come into its own, thus invoking soul forces within.

Perhaps dyslexics, with their deep, hidden talents, already bear within them an unconscious sense of the future evolution of the human race. Perhaps they have already exchanged the spirit of what is merely thought for that of direct vision. Perhaps they stand in bewilderment before letters as we would before Egyptian hieroglyphs because their souls are seeking direct revelations of the spirit.

Perhaps.

Certainly, at any rate, the three letters in a fixed form and sequence which compose d-o-g are not a direct manifestation of the creature designated by that name; nor even the thought of the word 'dog.' They are just the current social convention that we use to externally depict 'dog.' Letters are external life.

Nevertheless — and here I am contradicting neither my own 'heretical' comment above, nor the visionary statement of Rudolf Steiner — mastery of written communication remains indispensable (at least as far as we can see into the immediate future) not only as an aim of humanistic education but also as vital tool for meeting the challenges of the present and the future.

Language in written form must be understood and also expressed (that is, written) in an understandable way. For this reason our children must acquire literacy skills, even if, in my view, spelling in the future will assume a less important role than it has today. However, the techniques that children today and in the near future use to access the world of letters — before they are ever divided into dyslexics and non-dyslexics — need to change. There is no need for a 'battle' with letters.

If it proves possible to awaken in all children the dyslexic gifts of holistic, pictorial and non-verbal thinking in the depths of the soul, the process of learning to write can become a successful and satisfying phase of life and development for all. At the same time it can activate a wide range of other talents and mental, spiritual and emotional resources.

Other issues

I don't want to get side-tracked from my primary theme of examining the problems dyslexics have with written language, so I will only briefly touch on diverse possibilities for nurturing a range of different talents and gifts. Whether we are speaking of dyscalculia or attention deficit disorder (such as hyperactivity), a range of other 'developmental problems' or 'learning disorders' can be viewed from the perspective of Davis's findings — especially since they are often linked with dyslexia.

Research by the DDA (Davis Dyslexia Association) is already going well beyond 'pure' dyslexia to examine such tendencies. The appendix contains relevant contact addresses and bibliography references.

One example among many is the book *Beyond ADD — Hunting for Reasons in the Past and Present* by Thom Hartmann on the theme of ADD (attention deficit disorder). This was first previewed in the *Dyslexic Reader*, issue 9, spring 1997. Here he suggests other ways of looking at the problem, and thus other evaluation models for this 'abnormality', which in our culture is in such urgent need of treatment. Thom Hartmann reports:

In India a very different view of ADD has developed from the one commonly held in the US. During the monsoon season in 1993, I undertook a twelve-hour train journey through half the sub-continent in order to visit a small town close to the Bay of Bengal. In the same compartment sat various Indian businessmen and a doctor.

I was interested to find out how they saw ADD and I asked them: 'Are you familiar with a personality type such that the people concerned thirst for stimulation but at the same time have great difficulty in staying focused on anything? They hop as it were from career to career and sometimes also from one relationship to another, and never seem to get their feet properly on the ground.

'Oh yes, we know this type well,' said one of the men, and the others nodded in agreement.

'What do you call them?' I asked

'Very holy,' he replied. 'These are old souls close to the end of their karmic cycle.' Again the other three nodded in agreement, slightly more vehemently if anything, as if responding to my probing look.

'Old souls?' I asked, thinking this was after all a very strange way to describe what we regard as a deficiency.

'Yes,' said the doctor, 'in our religion we believe that the point of reincarnation is ultimately to liberate oneself from worldly constrictions and desires. In every life we pass through certain learning processes, until at last we are free of this earth and dissolve into the unified One — which you would call God. When a soul is close to the end of its thousands of incarnations it has to take several lives to do many, many things in order to disentangle the last few threads that still remain from past lives.'

'*Such a person is close to enlightenment,*' *added the first businessman. 'We have the highest respect for such individuals.*'

Ronald Davis also takes an outspoken view of the problems of autism (*see* the Davis Autism Approach, www.davisautism.com). Also interesting in this connection are the books by the professor of neurology Oliver Sacks, such as *The Man who Mistook His Wife for a Hat* and (specifically in connection with autism) *An Anthropologist on Mars.*

And last but not least: on December 9, 1997, in an article entitled 'Mozart's iridescence,' the magazine *die Zeit* reported on another 'colourful' aspect of human perceptive capacity, that of synaesthesia. People with this capacity can 'visually' perceive emotions, smells or tastes. Many also 'see' certain numbers, letters or tones as colours, for in this state the fixed boundaries between different sensory perceptions are erased.

Clearly all these different phenomena, and their causes and effects, should not be simply labelled 'disability,' 'disease' or 'disorder,' but instead we should retain our respect for the fact that others see the world in different ways.

If Ronald Davis's ideas led to nothing but this — cultivating new understanding for difference — this would be an important first step. And also wholly in accord with Rudolf Steiner's conviction:

The person of today who thinks materialistically can easily mock such things. He will regard it as a psychological epidemic and say that what comes from pathological minds should merely be disregarded.

I'd like to ask such a materialist what he would say if someone became mentally ill so that the psychiatrist had him sectioned in a lunatic asylum; and there, in his illumined state, he began to dream up the idea for a flying machine — something long desired by the human race — that was in fact practically feasible? People would not hesitate to accept this if it worked, without asking whether it came from a pathological mind.

Categorizing someone as 'sick' is no criterion. What is important is to test the content that arises from this person's psyche. The worst thing about the materialistic spirit of today is that it appeals to marginal considerations instead of invoking the power of truth. [57]

In other words, it is definitely worthwhile exploring new worlds of experience and knowledge.

But from here onwards I myself wish to focus as narrowly and specifically as possible on the realm of dyslexia: on problems with literacy. I will first draw on some interesting findings from modern brain physiology and then move on to some practical considerations relating to my theses.

This book can of course only offer food for thought: some 'parts of the puzzle' that came to my attention more or less accidentally as I read books and articles in connection with my work with dyslexics.

A Glimpse into Brain Physiology Research

A glimpse into recent brain physiology research is like looking through a gigantic telescope into infinity: behind every galaxy new, ever more distant systems are discovered, behind which in turn lie other unknown worlds. And what lies beyond them?[58]

The brain researcher Eccles is convinced that it will take hundreds of years before the brain can largely understand itself. The more we discover, the more we understand that we cannot yet fathom everything.

In daring to probe a little into this infinity, I am only taking a glimpse — a first, subjective and largely random glimpse, which makes absolutely no claim to having an overview of the secrets of the 100 billion or so synapses composing the cerebral nerve centres and neurone networks in our head. But should we refrain from looking and asking simply because we do not yet know everything?

Brain research — at least to the extent and speed with which it is undertaken today — is still a young science. Never before did knowledge about neurones and the brain, about perceptions and assimilation of sensory signals, multiply so rapidly as in the last decade of the twentieth century, declared the 'decade of the brain' by ex-American president George Bush senior. And since then the momentum has gathered even greater pace.

When the world's largest brain-research association, the Society for Neuroscience, celebrated its 25th anniversary in November 1995, around 20,000 scientists gathered in San Diego. Despite this, much of the research is still in its infancy, for even a presidential decree cannot compress into a single decade an undertaking that may still last 'hundreds of years' (according to Eccles).

At the same time we know a great deal more about brain processes and connections than we did twenty or thirty years ago. Or rather, we could know more if these research findings reached us in a comprehensible and applicable way, or if we knew how to access them. For instance, findings relating to the 'areas of responsibility' of both halves of the brain are particularly relevant to the dyslexia debate.

In order to pre-empt justified criticism that I am simplifying here, it is important to say that localization of 'areas of responsibility' in the brain which, between the sixties and eighties were regarded as proven and true of all people, is now disputed by various researchers; it must doubtless be seen in more differentiated terms than I can manage in what follows. In this respect too, people can't all be lumped together. Each person is different and their synapse connections will be individual. Steiner also speaks of 'footprints' in the brain that are configured individually in the course of learning to walk, to speak and to think. [59]

Nevertheless, sometimes it is useful to think in terms of a simplified account that represents the majority if not all, so as to better understand ourselves and recognize certain interconnections.

Since Leonardo da Vinci, at least, we have known that the brain has a right and a left half, which, in line with the ancient worldview, were called 'hemispheres' — and thus reflected the earth and the heavens. Knowledge of the degree of difference between these hemispheres, however, scarcely extended beyond the fact that two halves exist, just as we also have a left and a right ear.

In 1861, the French physician Paul Broca discovered the link between the left half of the body and the right half of the brain. Since then we know that the speech centre, called 'Broca's centre' after him, is situated in the left hemisphere in most people (roughly 98 per cent of right-handed people and 66 per cent of left-handed people). And at about the same time, the German physiologist Hermann von Helmholtz formulated the first theories about the connection between brain activities and consciousness, still unheard of at that time. But only since the 1860s did scientific knowledge grow of the radical specialization and difference in the mode of thinking of each half; and how each hemisphere augments and enhances the other and both are involved in our cognitive processes. Intuitive knowledge of it had long existed, though not (yet) amongst scientists, let alone educationalists and teachers. Artists and poets, however, had long had an inkling. In Rudyard Kipling's *Kim* for instance, the following passage appears:[60]

Something I owe to the soil that grew —
More to the life that fed —
But most to Allah Who gave me two
Separate sides to my head.

I would go without shirts or shoes,
Friends, tobacco or bread
Sooner than for an instant lose
Either side of my head.

I will come back to the question of why 'science' took a few years longer than artists to realize this; but finally, in 1973, the American brain researcher Professor Roger W. Sperry wrote:

The main theme to emerge ... is that there appear to be two modes of thinking, verbal and non-verbal, represented rather separately in left and right hemispheres, respectively, and that our educational system, as well as science in general, tends to neglect the non-verbal form of intellect. What it comes down to is that modern society discriminates against the right hemisphere. [61]

In 1981, Professor Sperry was awarded the Nobel Prize for Medicine for his brain research. In contrast, sixteen years later, the 'Interdisciplinary Committee of the Hessen Regional Dyslexia Association' took the following position in relation to Ronald Davis's book, *The Gift of Dyslexia* (quoted by R. Bergius):

Thus Davis distinguishes between verbal and non-verbal concepts. The 'verbal' is said to be the speech sound for a concept whereas the 'non-verbal' is the pictorial idea of it. This kind of distinction is unknown. The most one can do is distinguish between logical categories and so-called 'natural' concepts.

In his book, in fact, Ronald Davis did not in any way distinguish between verbal and non-verbal concepts but instead between the verbal and non-verbal formation of concepts — in other words between different modes of thinking. But no doubt the Interdisciplinary Committee would also have declared this distinction, which Sperry formulated in 1973, to be 'unknown.'

The difference between verbal and non-verbal modes of thinking which had started to 'crystallize out' for Professor Sperry was soon being described in an ever fuller and more differentiated way.

The functions of the hemispheres

Here are two slightly different examples of left-right models, which do however basically agree. They are by authors whose ideas I will return to later in more detail.

In her very interesting book *Unicorns are Real, a Right-Brained Approach to Learning,* Barbara Meister Vitale first gives an overview of hemisphere specialization:[62]

Left hemisphere (L mode):
Handwriting · symbols · language · reading · phonics · locating details and facts ·
talking and reciting · following directions · listening · auditory association

Right hemisphere (R mode):
Haptic awareness · spatial awareness · shapes and patterns · mathematical
computation · colour sensitivity · singing and music · art expression · creativity ·
visualization · feelings and emotions

She then cites examples of how left- or right-hemisphere modes of awareness manifest in children.[63] To illustrate this I will quote a passage that characterizes the domain of 'reality and imagination' and connects powerfully with the title of the book:

Left-hemispheric children can deal with reality, with the way things are. They can deal with the pictures and stories they are given in school. Left-hemispheric children are very much affected by the environment and will adjust to it. If something is presented to them, they will shift and react. That is the way they go through life. If something is not there for left-hemispheric children, it doesn't exist for them.

Right-hemispheric children will try to change the environment, to make it shift and react to meet their needs in any way they know how. This tendency often shows up as

Ricarda, aged 11: 'Unicorn'

behaviour problems in these children. They deal with fantasy, with imagery, with imagination. They are more comfortable creating from within.

I remember Kevin, who was always late for school. One morning, with big brown eyes turned upward, he announced: 'I met this unicorn that wanted directions to the nearest rainbow, and he promised me you wouldn't be mad.' That was the last straw. 'Kevin,' I yelled, 'you know unicorns aren't real!' With a look of complete indignation he yelled back, 'Unicorns are real!'

During the year I learned that, to Kevin, unicorns were very real.

As a teacher of drawing, Betty Edwards looks at everything from a somewhat different angle. In her book entitled *Drawing on the Right Side of the Brain,* she defines the hemispheres' modes of thinking as follows:[64]

L mode (left hemisphere)
- *Verbal: Using words to name, describe, define.*
- *Analytic: Figuring things out step-by-step and part-by-part.*
- *Symbolic: Using a symbol to stand for something.*
- *Abstract: Taking out a small bit of information and using it to represent the whole thing.*
- *Temporal: Keeping track of time, sequencing one thing after another.*
- *Rational: Drawing conclusions based on reason and facts.*
- *Logical: Drawing conclusions based on logic: one thing following another in logical order, for example, a mathematical theorem or a well-stated argument.*
- *Linear: Thinking in terms of linked ideas, one thought directly following another, often leading to a convergent conclusion.*

R mode (right hemisphere)
- *Non-verbal: Awareness of things, but minimal connection with words.*
- *Synthetic: Putting things together to form wholes.*
- *Concrete: Relating to things as they are, at the present moment.*
- *Analogic: Seeing likenesses between things; understanding metaphoric relationships.*
- *Non-temporal: Without a sense of time.*
- *Non-rational: Not requiring a basis of reason or facts; willingness to suspend judgment.*
- *Spatial: Seeing where things are in relation to other things, and how parts go together to form a whole.*
- *Intuitive: Making leaps of insight, often based on incomplete patterns, hunches, feelings, or visual images.*
- *Holistic: Seeing whole things all at once; perceiving the overall patterns and structures, often leading to divergent conclusions.*

All this, and probably much more (even if we allow for individual differences and shifts), falls into the domain of either the left or right side of our brain. Neither is more valuable or less dispensable than the other. Did nature perhaps endow us equally on both sides, and is our pronounced right-side dominance merely a consequence of the prevailing cultural norm? What effect, indeed, does any particular culture have on the development of dominance? I was struck by this recently when observing Egyptian sculptures: the representations of the body all express what I suspect to be an original equality of laterality. This gives them a static, non-dynamic quality, but at the same time they appear composed and well balanced. All step forward with the left foot whereas they hold their weapons, tools or offerings indiscriminately in their right and left hands.

Our Egyptian tour guide vehemently denied that this was accidental: gods, priests and pharaohs, he said, always put their left foot forward because they were taking a 'conscious' step, and in those times consciousness was considered to reside in the heart.

At some point in human history, on the journey from the Egyptian era through the Greek to the Roman, this changed. Right dominance came increasingly to the fore amongst the Romans. If you look at Roman sculptures you can see that the right leg is often placed forward, and the right arm or hand is the active one (see picture). What has happened here?

Usually we can discern a simultaneous development: written communication transformed from Egyptian hieroglyphs to Latin letters, from picture symbols to abstract sound identifiers. Whether the one brought about the other, or vice versa, is something the experts will have to decide. As far as I am concerned, however, there is a palpable connection between these two things.

With the Roman Empire, right-side dominance came to hold sway; and as one can see, the latter proved more lasting than the former. It still works right into our language: 'doing the right thing,' 'am I right to assume?' 'right and proper' and so on. 'Left' on the other hand gives us (via French) the word 'gauche' which means 'awkward' or 'lacking in tact.'

It is not only in language that we still find traces of discrimination against everything to do with 'left': it encompasses superstition (for instance, when a black cat runs across your path from the left), social etiquette (shaking hands with the 'good' rather than 'wrong' hand) and even politics — originally parties of a socialist leaning were allocated seats on the 'bad side,' on the left, in early parliaments.

Oddly enough, the only attribute ensconced firmly on the left in our right-leaning world is, as ever, the left hemisphere: the half of the brain responsible for our 'right and proper' (but not right-brained) abilities.

In this left-brain, right-dominated world it is hardly surprising that every effort to urge those responsible for education and culture to acknowledge the equality of both halves of the brain, and the value of enabling people to draw on both hemispheres, encounters enormous obstacles.

If right-brain abilities have degenerated to the extent that their qualities have become self-negating, how can a left-brained society be persuaded to acknowledge this wordless, artistic, creative, intuitive, ineffable something in us? Or to accept that not all people possess the same, standard mode of thinking and perception?

In relation to the daunting nature of this task, Jerome Brunner says:

There is something antic about creating, although the enterprise be serious. And there is a matching antic spirit that goes with writing about it, for if ever there was a silent process, it is the creative one. [65]

And yet long before Ronald Davis, the phenomenon of non-verbal thinking was, without any scientific support from brain research, certainly known to some, including some who are very well known.

The phenomenon of non-verbal thinking

In 1945, Albert Einstein said:

The words or the language as they are written or spoken do not seem to play any role in my mechanism of thought. The psychical entities which seem to serve as elements in thought are certain signs and more or less clear images which can be 'voluntarily' reproduced and combined.

And George Orwell wrote, in *Politics and the English language* (1946):

In prose, the worst thing one can do with words is surrender to them. When you think of a concrete object, you think wordlessly, and then, if you want to describe the thing you have been visualizing you probably hunt about until you find the exact words that seem to fit it.

When you think of something abstract you are more inclined to use words from the start, and unless you make a conscious effort to prevent it, the existing dialect will come rushing in and do the job for you, at the expense of blurring or even changing your meaning. Probably it is better to put off using words as long as possible and get one's meaning as clear as one can through pictures and sensations.

This friendly advice to keep away from words for as long as possible was something which Victor Hugo took to heart — or rather prefigured — as early as 1862. And he did so in the most radical way. According to the *Guinness Book of Records*, he conducted the shortest correspondence in human history. After the publication of his book *Les Misérables,* he travelled to the country, where uncertainty about the success of his volume left him no peace. He therefore wrote to his publisher: '?' By return of post he received the most satisfactory answer: '!' Nothing had been said but it was wholly comprehensible.

Steiner also repeatedly speaks of the 'pictorial' nature of thoughts: 'But we have to imagine that even in thinking activity we are only involved in pictorial activity ...'[66]

In explaining the life of soul and spirit as a complex rhythm of sympathy and antipathy, he describes concept formation in the following terms:

Once you have undergone this whole procedure, once you have imagined pictorially, have cast this back in memory, and retain hold of the pictorial element, then the concept arises.[67]

And he criticizes mere thinking in words in the following vivid terms:

This is what must become so endlessly necessary for humanity: that people make efforts to enter into reality. Nowadays people think almost entirely in words, rather than in realities ...

They do not connect any concepts with the way they fetch things from reality ... People believe they understand reality to the greatest possible degree; but when they start to speak, only the emptiest husks of words come out.[68]

In this context Steiner is responding in particular to comments by politicians of his day; yet the 'word husks' of politicians (and others) have not gained much substance in the intervening period. In fact the contrary may be true, as a news report dated May 24, 1998 illustrates rather well, if grotesquely:

London. According to the environmental organization Greenpeace, radioactive waste has been discharged from the Thorp plutonium reprocessing plant at the Sellafield nuclear power site ... A spokesperson for the operator of the Sellafield site, British Nuclear Fuels (BNFL), dismissed the claims by Greenpeace. There was no leak. It was just a little fluid that had escaped from a damaged pipe.

You actually have to read this twice! Have things reached the stage where we are no longer able to picture what a leak is? No doubt the operators of Sellafield would be pleased if this were so. If we no longer know that a leak is a place in a damaged pipe from which fluid escapes, then we could perhaps accept that no leak occurred. But if attempts are made to use 'word husks' to pull the wool over our eyes about tangible things, what about abstract concepts?

In her book *Stroh im Kopf?* (A Head Full of Straw?) the psychologist, journalist and author Vera F. Birkenbihl shows how easily we take refuge in abstractions. Though her book focuses on the German language specifically, it no doubt also applies to English. She ascertains that two 'levels' of language have evolved: a 'simple' level for everyone, and a 'higher' one for educated people. The latter aims to 'distinguish' the user, for example as follows:

The relative efficiency of accumulated communication substrates based on the functional relation between the absolute capacity of the recipient and the quantitative Thesaurus of offered information. [69]

Even reading this twice is unlikely to help much! In Birkenbihl's view, this author does not even wish to inform his readers, but simply to make an impression. Otherwise he could have expressed himself as follows: 'It is well worth considering that there are two laws at work in the successful art of conversation.'

The brain as organ of learning

It is well worth considering Vera F. Birkenbihl and her publications, books and games. She is the director of the Institute for Brain Friendly Procedures in Odelzhausen near Munich, and gives lectures and seminars — primarily to the finance and business sectors. She coined the term 'brain friendly' in 1990. Brain-friendly learning means, according to her, that for optimum learning a piece of information should be grasped simultaneously by both the left and right hemispheres. I will come back to this.

I encountered Vera F. Birkenbihl in the form of the Ravensburger 'THINK' brain-training game. In the accompanying handbook she writes:

While all people are born with a brain, education and training processes have denied most of them the chance to develop their huge potential. Typical symptoms of this lack are a (supposedly) poor memory, concentration problems, fear of learning etc. ... For instance you'll probably know that adults mostly lose in memory games with children, because the latter use their brain intuitively and thus optimally.

In connection with dyslexia, it is interesting to see what she attributes the left-brain emphasis of school learning to historically:

School learning is decisively based on trials conducted by Ebbinghaus. Over 100 years ago the latter showed how optimum learning occurs through 'nonsense' syllables (similar to rote learning of words about which one as yet knows nothing).

His idea was that once a pupil knows the Latin word 'tabula' he will learn the English word 'table' much more easily than a pupil who has no knowledge of a Romance language.

In order to exactly determine how people learn, one has to take material which carries no prior associations for any of the test subjects. This is why he resorted to nonsense syllables (such as puk, flam, bif etc.). After thousands of trials 'the results were clear!' And this is the basis of the learning and forgetting curves which are still used today.

The good Ebbinghaus and his followers overlooked the fact, however, that our brain is an organ of learning par excellence— but for useful things, and thus information which either ensures our survival or which at least interests us. [70]

The old Ebbinghaus method strikes me as familiar: in dyslexia diagnosis, in fact, such tasks are still set today. To ascertain sound differentiation deficiencies and attention deficits, children are supposed to repeat nonsense words and syllables. But because they are not used to thinking so one-sidedly, many will activate their pictorial thinking and disorientation function in order to discover some meaning in the word.

But since, inevitably, this will not produce any solution, they remain disorientated and thus make mistakes when repeating. If one takes Ebbinghaus as a parameter for learning success, one can really only conclude that these children are failing in relation to typical school learning. But would they still fail if we offered them 'brain-friendly' material?

Vera F. Birkenbihl heard from the mother of a dyslexic child — whose child had already made some progress based on suggestions contained in her books — about the child's enormous step forward since discovering the Davis method. Impressed by Davis and his experiences, Birkenbihl then wrote the foreword for the revised edition of his book *The Gift of Dyslexia*. Thus a connection was suddenly made in a chain of ideas that I had only observed from a distance.

If our brain has the capacity and potential to be a learning organ par excellence, yet if, despite this excellence, learning difficulties arise, or more specifically, problems in learning literacy skills, one of the reasons for this must surely be the huge BUT in the quote by Birkenbihl: precisely the thing which the good Ebbinghaus (and others) overlooked: 'The brain is indisputably an excellent organ of learning, BUT for useful things: information which either ensures our survival or at least interests us.'

Yet what on earth is useful and what is interesting? This is easy to say in relation to ensuring our survival, because it is common to all of us. But as regards interesting information, this will vary from individual to individual, and has a great deal to do with hemisphere dominance. The dyslexic's mode of thinking is hard put to develop interest in the intrinsically non-pictorial letters of our alphabet.

To implant such an interest from without becomes increasingly difficult since today we have access to a more or less unlimited wealth of information media. By these means a dyslexic can satisfy his thirst for knowledge pictorially and thus a thousand times quicker than circuitously via written words. But this does not, of course, imply a learning deficiency of the brain. It may, rather, be a lack of learning or training due to neglect of right-brain potential by commonly applied teaching methods.

Betty Edwards expresses her criticism of school learning as follows:

Even today, though educators are increasingly concerned with the importance of intuitive and creative thought, school systems in general are still structured in the left-hemisphere mode ...

The right brain — the dreamer, the artificer, the artist — is lost in our school system and goes largely untaught. [71]

In his dissertation on the problem of one-sided, left-hemisphere-oriented school learning, Gerhard Huhn says:

It is a matter of having or not having respect for the human being's universal and as yet largely unknown potential; for what can unfold anew in every single individual; it is a matter of regard for the creative principle innate in us ... [72]

For this reason we should look back to the experiences of great artists and scientists, but also to the knowledge of eastern philosophies (e.g. Taoism and Zen Buddhism) in order to gain access to the initially paradoxical and (of course) 'illogical' opportunities for nurturing right-hemisphere activities. [73]

I am convinced that the key to awakening brain-friendly interest rather than dominance-related lack of interest lies in our own artistic potential — and not, to name just one currently very widespread neurological approach, in a general schooling of the senses or similar, such as Jean Ayres urges. In her book *Sensory Integration and the Child* she suggests that difficulties at school are connected with a lack of sensory-motor integration.

Very briefly, Ayres' thesis, as I understand it, is that the brain does not properly process external sensory perceptions (vision, hearing, balance, touch and movement) and that therefore these senses are in need of better training.

Thinking and perceiving

I certainly won't hide the fact that such an approach seems, at first glance, to be supported by Rudolf Steiner. In a lecture given on April 16, 1923, and speaking about the importance of fine motor skills, balance and learning to walk for speech development, he said:

You will see that if a child walks sloppily, he will not speak with the right pauses between one sentence and the next, but instead the sentences will all merge into each other.

And if a child doesn't learn to make harmonious movements with his arms, his speech will be raspy and not well-formed.

Likewise, if you don't get a child to sense the life in his fingers, he will not acquire a sense for speech modulation and inflections.

But listen carefully: who is Rudolf Steiner addressing when he says 'you?' Surely not teachers and therapists of children with learning difficulties, for in the next sentence he adds: 'All this relates to the period while the child is learning to walk and speak.' [74]

Walking and speaking. According to Steiner, thinking is only the third developmental step to be completed. Just as human evolution took place in the three stages of walking — speaking — thinking, so the same applies to the development of each individual.

But if the right-brained emphasis of the dyslexics' mode of thinking leads to their problems, then these problems must, clearly, be the result and not the cause of this thinking. Whatever sensory-motor exercises are used to treat dyslexia, even if they achieve positive results, they do not go to the root of the problem and its alleviation, for this lies in thinking itself.

But what criteria can one use to judge a mode of thinking that is different from the average, and declare that it needs modification? 'Normal' and 'abnormal?' What is normal? If the majority of people are normal, then you can say that in our latitudes all brown-haired people are normal and all blondes abnormal. The distortion of sensory perceptions that are common to the majority of people (which is what Davis calls disorientation) is certainly 'normal' in the right-brain processing mode. It can even be particularly desirable and worth nurturing, although our left-brain, rational sciences do not affirm this. Artists do though. For example, Carlo Carra says in *The Quadrant of the Spirit:*

I know perfectly well that only in happy instants am I lucky enough to lose myself in my work. The painter-poet feels that his true immutable essence comes from that invisible realm that offers him an image of eternal reality ... I feel that I do not exist in time, but that time exists in me. I can also realize that it is not given to me to solve the mystery of art in an absolute fashion. Nonetheless, I am almost brought to believe that I am to get my hands on the divine. [75]

And of course experiences of this inestimable sort, beyond normal perception, were not unknown to Rudolf Steiner:

Try immersing yourself in the plant so that you feel how gravity passes down into the earth via the root, how the power of blossoming unfolds above. Share in the experience of blossoming and fruiting ...

Try submerging yourself entirely in the external world, so that you are taken up by it. You awaken again as though from a faint. But now you no longer receive abstract thoughts but imaginations. You receive images. And materialism no longer recognizes any kind of knowledge in these images which you receive.

People say that knowledge has to proceed in abstract, logical concepts. But what if the world is not suited to revealing itself in logic's abstract concepts!

If, for example, the world were a work of art, we would have to grasp it artistically not logically; then logic would merely be there as a necessary discipline — but it would not help us understand the world itself any better.[76]

In pictorial images, says Steiner, materialism no longer recognizes knowledge — or rather any knowledge that proceeds in abstract, logical concepts.

But dyslexics think primarily in images! How therefore can they arrive at an understanding of something that cannot be more abstract, of the world of letters?

The following sentence is also one worth pondering: 'But what if the world is not suited to revealing itself in logic's abstract concepts!' I'd like to engage with this sentence a little more and 'translate' it freely in a way that accords with my sense of things:

Yes, if the thinking of dyslexics is not of a kind to reveal itself to logic's abstract concepts — if a child thinks in a right-brained way — then we must meet it via the right brain and not logically; then logic is merely useful as a discipline that *we* use ourselves. But we will not understand the child at all through logic.

Dyslexics naturally have insights — many and profound ones which often leave us left-brainers miles behind. The materialistic perspective does not necessarily recognize these instincts, as they do not fit into logic's abstract concepts.

Parents of dyslexic children could recount endless instances of this capacity if our materialistic world did not immediately label them cranks. Subjectively their experiences might no doubt be regarded as interesting or astonishing 'encounters of the third kind,' but in fact they are more likely to be assigned to the realm of fable. In these situations it helps to hear observations by others which show one's own experiences in a far less cranky light. Thus Vera F. Birkenbihl reports in her book:

There is another interesting aspect which I haven't mentioned so far. It is highly likely that so-called paranormal capacities (telepathy, telekinesis, second sight etc.) also lie in the right brain ... For decades now, at least, I have used telepathy exercises in some of my seminars (evening courses, voluntary participants) and repeatedly found that the typical, rational left-brainer has most difficulty with them.[77]

Werner Holzapfel writes something similar:

It is possible that the primarily negative characterization could be modified by seeing that dyslexic children possess a striking understanding for spiritual ideas. I believe that I have observed this in the cases known to me.[78]

Laterality and dominance

Let us now return to our initial thesis: if a child thinks in a right-brained mode, we must approach him in a right-brain way.

For physically visible dominance, right-brained thinking does not automatically mean that children are left-handed. Mostly they are ambidextrous or have crossed laterality (right hand/left foot). Only a few are clearly left-handed.

Here, once again, it is Rudolf Steiner who builds a bridge between 'cranky,' 'paranormal' or 'spiritual' abilities and the question of dominance and laterality. It is undisputed that Steiner advocated getting left-handers to convert to writing with the right hand, which, interestingly, he justifies with reference to the findings of Broca, who located the speech centre in the left hemisphere;[79] but here too it is well worth taking a closer look at his more specific references to this: [80]

Yes, in general one will find that the children who have a more spiritual disposition can write equally well either with the left or right hand. But children who are more materialistic will become idiotic if they write with both hands.

There is a real reason why right-handedness is prevalent. In this materialistic age, children can become idiotic if they use both hands alternately.

Under certain circumstances this can be a real cause for concern in relation to all the things requiring reason; but not at all in drawing. It's fine to let them draw with both hands.

Clearly then, Rudolf Steiner is not suggesting that all left-handed or ambidextrous children must be indiscriminately turned into right-handers, even if, initially, we may be staggered at the suggestion that materialistic children 'become idiotic.'

And he is also distinguishing carefully between writing with both hands and doing other things such as drawing — which for him is something different, and does not belong to the things that embody reason; it does not therefore have its seat in the left hemisphere but in a different mode of perception. I do not know to what extent I can simply transpose Steiner into my particular concerns. But we need to find new words to engage in comprehensible dialogue about the breadth of Steiner's ideas, making them relevant for contemporary life, rather than simply cringing because we can't make sense of them.

When are children materialistic? What is the materialistic age we hear about so often? Certainly, at any rate, it is something that needs to be overcome, that must (and will) make way for something new — perhaps also in the therapeutic field.

In future, in the light of brain research findings, we may view many of our current diagnosis and therapy approaches differently. Maybe we will no longer try to force children with left- or bi-laterality — whether they show 'learning difficulties' or not — into a one-sided, 'correct' and usually right-sided dominance (hand, eye, foot) which, in the prevailing view, is meant to have developed by the age of seven. Currently a lot of back-up support is needed if bilaterality or crossed dominance has not been overcome by that age.

Perhaps Audrey McAllen is also simply still entangled in 'materialistic thinking' when she advocates a one-sided preference for the left hemisphere — especially where there are learning difficulties:

Because no training is given, like guidance in using the right side of the body while dressing (the right arm into the coat first, the right shoe onto the right foot first) many children become confused during this time ... If the school child is still ambidextrous, we shall find it revealed when we compare the child's Simple Dominance with his Handedness Pattern. Unconfirmed sidedness is the basis of the cross dominance which can inhibit learning faculties.

Dominance, the preferred use of one side of the body, is usually attained around the age of seven, after the vertical midline barrier is integrated and the ambidextrous stage is complete. At this time there is a spurt of growth in the left hemisphere of the brain and both hemispheres have developed their holistic and localized functions. [81]

But what if this isn't the case? What if the diagnosed 'growth spurt' of the left hemisphere is not a naturally occurring, evolutionary process but one induced by society and culture due to the fact that the child has been born into and educated in a left-brain-oriented world? In this case the 'growth spurt' may only be a block that hinders development of right-brain capacities.

Gerhard Haberland assumes that most people are naturally bilateral or ambidextrous, and states:

Due to education and the right-handed emphasis, a considerable proportion of ambidextrous children, and those with a slight left-handed tendency, become accustomed to preferring the right hand, and experience themselves as being right-handed, despite still retaining left-handed skills.

Genetic disposition thus seems to play a role in the development of dominance; laterality is innate and, according to Haberland, distributed across the population in line with the Gauss error-function graph below:

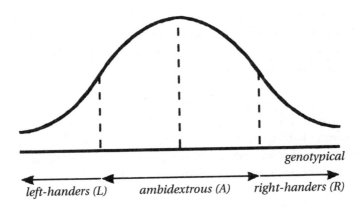

genotypical

left-handers (L)   ambidextrous (A)   right-handers (R)

Haberland sees the problems of dyslexics as due to the fact they run counter to the cultural norm and thus almost inevitably collide with it. As a rule, dyslexics do not have a clearly distinguished dominance, but an ambidextrous predisposition, or have retained this.

This has repeatedly been noticed, and is also to be found in various neurophysiological trials, which Sally P. Springer and Georg Deutsch refer to in *Left Brain, Right Brain*. For instance, in four out of seven cases, autopsies on dyslexic adults found an unusual symmetry of the *planum temporale* — an area of the brain which normally (in 70 per cent of people) is a third larger on the left side of the brain than on the right side. In four of those examined, the *planum temporale* was equal in size on both sides: the left was not as 'small' as the right, however, but the right was as large as the left.

We do not necessarily have to resort to autopsies to gain insight into brain organization and its structure. The living brain also reveals some of its secrets. In studies using magnetic resonance tomographs, 70 per cent of dyslexics examined show planum symmetry, whereas only 30 per cent of control subjects have this.

In addition, female dyslexics, followed by male dyslexics, have been shown to possess the largest cross-section of the *corpus callosum*, the largest nerve fibre tract in the brain, which unites the two hemispheres. People with normal literacy skills show the smallest *corpus callosum*.

Such enlarged *corpus callosums* (accompanying pronounced ambidexterity) has also been discovered in musicians, chiefly those who play classical keyboard and string instruments and start their musical training before the age of seven.

Currently no final conclusion has been reached about the role of the *corpus callosum* in higher cognitive processes. What is clear is that it is very complex; and one thing seems certain: the *corpus callosum* completes its quickest growth during foetal development, doubles its size between birth and the end of the second year, and subsequently grows only a little, reaching its maximum size by around the age of twenty-five. [82]

Betty Edwards, who locates 'completion' of dominance in the tenth year, has found that most adults in western cultures never progress beyond the level of artistic capacity that they achieve by the age of nine or ten. And based on this she makes the following comparison:

If we were to attach a label to this disability in the way that educators have attached the label dyslexia *to reading problems, we might call the problem* dyspictoria *or* dysartistica *or some such term. But no one has done so because drawing is not a vital skill for survival in our culture, whereas speech and reading are.* [83]

Here, I'd like to mention an observation which for me interestingly contextualized some of the aspects of dyslexia we have so far considered — learning difficulties, dominance, brain research, the Davis method, and Betty Edwards also, whom I first discovered because of this 'case.' In thinking about the problem of dyslexia it is not necessarily a self-evident thing to study a book about drawing.

I wished neither to learn to draw nor to teach it, but was induced to do so by a fifteen-year-old girl who came to me with huge difficulties at school. When I asked her what she would like to do better in future, she said 'draw better.' Drawing was what she was best at.

This led me to Betty Edwards, from whom I have since learned a great deal — even to draw better. And in helping this girl, I was able to include Edwards's exercises.

Although she did not necessarily appear to be dyslexic, she mainly needed help with reading and writing. She read 'automatically' — in other words she could not absorb any of the content of what she read; she excluded all the ideas contained in the text. After our 'orientation session,' I got her to form the alphabet capitals in plasticine, as Davis suggested. When she was about to name the letters and simultaneously touch them, I observed the following: the letters lay spread over the whole table on both sides of her, to her left and right. She began with her left hand but when she reached a position in front of her she always changed to the right hand. She never crossed the midline. I interpreted this to mean that she always only activated one half of the brain when relating to letters, and did not integrate the two. This was also demonstrated by her 'one-sided' way of reading.

I am aware that there are many physical exercises that can lead to crossing the midline (especially in the field of educational kinesiology), but despite this I simply carried on with the next task. At the same time as touching and naming the letters, she was to form a clear image of the letter in her mind's eye. I was astonished to see that she could now cross the midline without any problem.

Could this mean that there is a 'physical' manifestation when we give the brain a 'brain-friendly' task — such as here, for instance, when combining speech with picturing? In the case of this girl, as far as reading is concerned, the third stage of Davis's Spell-Reading method worked very well indeed. (See Ronald Davis's book *The Gift of Dyslexia* for a detailed description of the Spell-Reading method.)

In my view, training a bodily or hemisphere dominance to work unilaterally cannot be the way to make learning easier for children. Apart from the fact that this too often proves unsuccessful, it amounts to almost criminal neglect of children's innate potential, and at best will only condition them for our modern type of school learning. Barbara Meister Vitale sums it up succinctly:

We will begin to understand how the two hemispheres work together to give the individual a holistic view of his natural environment ... This integration creates an intelligence far greater than the sum of its parts. It is an intelligence that exists beyond specialization and beyond the individual modes of processing present in each hemisphere. It is this intelligence that is the unknown. It is the intelligence that invents, creates and involves. We may never understand this elusive concept, but we must keep trying. We must give children of the world a chance to reach their greatest heights! [84]

Much of the 'learning difficulties' and 'challenging behaviour' that we find today is caused by the fact that such children have *more* capacities, but for that very reason also *more* predisposition for confusion — for instance, more difficulties than others in deciding between two things. Below is a short story by a thirteen-year-old dyslexic relating to the word 'more':

mehr

*Heute fahre ich ans Meer.
Ich habe mehr Gepeck mit
als alle anderen. Als wir
angekommen waren wolten wir
sofort ins Meer, ich hatte mehr
Badeanzüge mit als alle anderen.
Deshalb kond ich nicht swimmen
weil ich mich nicht entscheiden
konte welchen ich anzihen sol.
Am Abend wolten wir in die
Disko ich hatte mehr Klamatten
mit als alle andern. Also kante
ich nicht mit weil ich mich nicht
entscheiden konte was ich anzihen
sol. Das Meer ist da!*

Today I am going to the seea
I v have more luggig with me
than all the others. when When we
got there we wonted
to go into the sea, I had more
bathing costums with me than all the others.
That's why I cold not swim
because I coud not decide
which one to put on.
In the evening we wonted to go to the
disco I had more cloths
with me than all the others. So I cold
not go with them as I cold not
decide what I shoud put on. The sea is ...

It seems to me that the only right way is to help them to connect their many different talents, or to learn to use their hemispheres in an integrated way. The task consists of recognizing these talents in children, even if we ourselves do not (or do not yet, or no longer) possess them; and to offer them schooling where they can learn to practise their full, bilateral capacities.

This 'new' type of teaching does not however need to be re-invented. I am convinced that it is already there in a useable and convincing form if one looks carefully at Rudolf Steiner's art of education.

This, at least, is how I understand his differentiated comments on the theme of 'unilaterality/bilaterality', in a lecture he gave on May 7, 1920:

Here I return to a question I have been asked, which is of great significance, and relates to left-handedness or ambidexterity.

You see, it is quite right in general to go beyond what has become a general human custom, right-handedness, which is used in learning to write and other skills one needs in life, by making the left hand more skilful. In a certain sense this is quite justified.

But when one discusses such things, the debate will only be fruitful if one also has deeper insight into human life.

If we live towards an age in which people will awaken their full humanity, in which our abstract understanding, so well developed today, will be enhanced by a culture of the heart, of feeling and will activity, then things can be discussed in a quite different way from what is usually possible.

If people continue to be educated as they are today, so that they stay stuck in abstractions — materialism is, after all, something that gets stuck in abstractions, and fails to apply spiritual understanding to the material world — then one will find after a while that developing the ability to write equally well with both hands will lead to a certain degree of feeble-mindedness. The way we are as human beings today is somewhat connected with the fact that we use the right hand considerably more than the left hand ...

I would not mention these things at all if I hadn't researched them very thoroughly, and if I hadn't, for example, tested and tried out what it means to use the left hand. Once one has developed capacities to observe people, then one can also try things out and discover what it means to use the left hand.

Using the left hand is beneficial once one has acquired a certain independence of soul and spirit from the body; but in the current state of dependency on the body which modern human beings have today, a huge upheaval occurs in the body itself if one uses the left hand in the same way as the right for such things as writing ...

The method of education which first applies the educational principles we have been discussing, can then also use ambidexterity. Modern culture must not simply abstractly adopt use of both hands. Such things can only, of course, be based on experience. But statistics would go a long way to proving what I have said here. [85]

This is the decisive passage which encourages me to ask whether it is always advisable to try to convert those who are clearly ambidextrous to the standard right-handedness, or whether we would do better to apply Rudolf Steiner's educational principles instead, making use of ambidexterity.

Holistic Capacities

Today people ask themselves the abstract question: how should we develop the child's abilities? But we need to be clear that we first have to know the capacities of the growing person if the abstract phrase about 'developing his abilities' is to have any tangible meaning. [86]

We first have to know the child's capacities, says Steiner, before we can start developing them. We can't simply set about teaching or using therapeutic interventions.

What happens when a child comes to school? Until then, he will have automatically developed the innate wealth of his two hemispheres in a natural way, and will have done so enormously fast. Now, as things start getting 'serious,' school learning breaks over the child's head, demanding and promoting left-hemisphere abilities.

Depending on a child's individual developmental process, this is when the first major loss of motivation can occur, simply because learning suddenly becomes so much slower. What was previously soaked up like a sponge is now pumped in. And during the process it is all too easy for the right-hemisphere learning abilities to dwindle — as Betty Edwards shows us in relation to drawing, and Vera Birkenbihl in relation to memory games.

This withering of capacities is not recognised by children or teachers as a 'loss' because traditional schooling normally 'functions' successfully. Even if children learn, perhaps, with less enthusiasm and more slowly than they would naturally, they are fashioned into functioning left-dominant thinkers, achieve higher school grades, gain academic honours and soon form yet another left-brain-dominant generation of 'brain geeks' rather than holistic 'brain owners.'

In relation to this, in an interview with the magazine *Ab 40*, Ronald Davis once said:

The education system doesn't understand much about the actual learning process ... Teaching is no longer an art, unfortunately ... Most teachers today are learning facilitators ... They are a product of the same system they're involved in when teaching. This has been going on for generations now.

But what did Rudolf Steiner say — over 80 years ago now — about the 'actual learning process,' the absorption or pumping in, as I called it just now?

We have to be able to educate so that predisposition and potential is created which we ourselves don't have. But this means that the human being in front of us has something which we as carers or teachers simply cannot begin to grasp. This is something we should regard with the profoundest respect, and which should develop through the art of education without us imposing on our charges an image of our own abilities. [87]

I am not the first person to draw a clear parallel between Rudolf Steiner's educational ideas and the concept of brain-friendly learning, introduced decades later by Vera Birkenbihl.

In his provocative dissertation on the risks of modern curricula for children's unhampered development, for example, Gerhard Huhn wrote in 1990:

Rudolf Steiner's Waldorf education, which originated in German-speaking countries but has now spread internationally, is a very comprehensive holistic education concept which can now look back on several decades of experience in using alternative educational methods and an entirely different way of handling the process of education. Many elements of this concept, in development since 1919, are in striking harmony with demands for 'brain-friendly' teaching arising from recent brain research. [88]

At this point it would be lovely to lean back and whole-heartedly praise this ideal form of schooling — if it were not for the fact that the daily reality of Waldorf schools is also beset with problems: teachers are faced with unmotivated pupils, and intelligent children with difficulties; learning foreign languages early (or at least at the right time, comparatively) is likewise fraught with problems.

The discrepancy between what is and what ought to be at Waldorf schools cannot be glossed over with the blithe assertion that theory and practice are two different things. In my view, the cause lies in what was referred to above: that our prevailing culture also 'hinders' teachers at Waldorf schools, with the result that their holistic skills are often only partially developed and trained.

Perhaps we would come one step closer to attaining the ideal if there were more teachers whose right-hemisphere abilities were more strongly developed.

It is evident, however, that people who think predominantly using right-hemisphere modes are often not the ones who become teachers in the first place. They tend to choose professions where they can use or reveal their special talents — as craftsmen, technicians, artists or architects.

If, especially as a dyslexic, you have waded your way laboriously through a left-brain-dominated schooling system as a child, you are unlikely to want to 'maltreat' children in turn by making them learn to read and write. Thus the vital task of education remains 'by nature' the preserve of teachers who, though highly motivated, loving and concerned, are simply untrained in (or trained to suppress?) right-hemisphere thinking.

There are only a few examples of a child who once had learning difficulties going on later to become a teacher. The teacher Barbara Meister Vitale, whom I have already quoted several times, is one of these exceptions. She relates that she was a child with 'learning difficulties' and only learned to read at the age of twelve. You can find more about her unusual and impressive career in her autobiography *Free Flight*, (Jalmar Press, 1986) which offers 'encouragement for all who think and live more intuitively than logically, more chaotically than orderly, and more imaginatively than reality-based.' But whether and when this example will make an impression on the schooling system is something I cannot predict.

Since we cannot assume, therefore, that school-age children with strong right-brain tendencies have teachers with strong right-brain gifts, other adults — whether parents, teachers or therapists — must work to acknowledge that the right-hemisphere gifts that exist, undeveloped, in all of us are of equal value to the left-hemisphere gifts that are nurtured. We can then recognize and use them in others, and train them in ourselves.

One of Rudolf Steiner's fundamental requirements of the first Waldorf teachers was that they should always start with their pupils rather than with themselves. Sadly, he only had six years in which to supervise the realization of his truly brilliant educational ideas (which Huhn believes he formulated intuitively); and often he did this from a distance rather than being continuously present himself in the school's daily life.

Certainly, however, he was not always best pleased at the way his educational ideals were implemented during his lifetime. Steiner's comments on early Waldorf practice are sometimes very critical indeed (cf. *Faculty Meetings with Rudolf Steiner*).

Would things have developed differently if he could have supervised his school for longer? I do not know. Nevertheless, for me the basic approach of the Waldorf School remains the ideal form of brain-friendly learning, drawing on (and acknowledging!) the potential of both hemispheres.

To make it into an ideal education for all — whether dyslexic or not — we should not concern ourselves with occasional shortcomings in daily practice but instead look to the roots from which the Waldorf school first grew over eighty years ago.

Gerhard Huhn was struck by the correlation between the concept of the Waldorf School and the theory of brain-friendly learning; I in turn have been struck by the correlation between the findings of Ronald Davis's dyslexia research and brain research in general, on the one hand, and on the other my own experiences of working with dyslexics' special mode of thinking, learning and perceiving, with Rudolf Steiner's educational theories.

In what follows I will give examples of these connections, though I am sure that many, many others could be found. Please take these merely as stimuli for your own further thoughts and research.

Brain-friendly Learning

I will start with an experiment conceived by Vera Birkenbihl. Please learn the following lines by heart:

Twolegs sits on threelegs and eats a oneleg. Along comes a fourlegs and takes the oneleg away from twolegs. Twolegs takes the threelegs and throws it at the fourlegs. [89]

Was it easy? Did you learn it quickly?

If you found it easy to learn, you probably made a picture for each of the 'legs' — which makes the text immediately accessible. Without images underlying the words it would remain a tortuous nonsense task.

But most likely you imagined a person sitting on a stool eating a chicken leg, and a dog who comes by and snatches it, at which the person hits the dog with the stool.

This mode of 'noting something' is what Vera Birkenbihl calls 'brain-friendly learning.' Information is absorbed simultaneously by the left hemisphere (speech) and the right hemisphere (image). By this means it reaches our long-term memory without much need for repetition. Not only does this speed things up, it also means we retain such information for considerably longer. I am sure you will still be able to repeat the paragraph you just learned next week.

In order to learn as well as possible, therefore, we have to invoke our capacity to think in images. Vera Birkenbihl says, 'As regards the word "picture," please take it literally: one places something before the mind's eye in order to observe it."[90]

Literal picturing, leading to activation of the right hemisphere, plays, in my view, a key role for brain-friendly literacy teaching.

For Rudolf Steiner at least, pictorial thinking was an entirely self-evident and natural precondition for successful learning, since he himself probably only learned by this means. This becomes clear from the following conversation with a Waldorf teacher:

X: The children in my Class Six [age eleven/twelve] have a poor memory. It must be an error in my teaching.

Steiner: You can't say that all the children's memories are poor.

X: The children don't retain things. They have no clear pictures, for example of Egypt.

Steiner: How do you try to teach pictorial thinking? (Geography teaching is now the subject of discussion.) ... The children recall the pyramids and obelisks. You have to ask yourself here whether you have really gone through everything in careful sequence, so as to give all the children a picture of the actual location of Egypt; so that they don't have any gaps in their ideas relating to it.

If one simply isolates Egypt, and the child has no sense or picture of how he would get from here to Egypt — if he has no three-dimensional picture — then it's quite possible for these things to bypass the memory. Perhaps one needs to ensure that every detail has been covered so that the children have an entirely graphic picture and no gaps in their idea of the location of Egypt in relation to where they are.

The child will know something about pyramids and obelisks without knowing they are located in Egypt. It is very important to consider whether all these things, which lead to complete pictures and ideas, have really been covered.

Do you just get the children to draw a picture of Africa? Perhaps one should also always get them to draw a map of Europe or other adjoining areas as well as the particular country you are studying, to give them an overview and context.[91]

How important 'complete pictures and ideas' can be is also demonstrated by one of Barbara Meister Vitale's learning strategies, which she developed for those she considers 'right-hemisphere' children. These include dyslexic children, and those with numeracy and attention deficit difficulties.

She tells of a child who had been pigeon-holed as having a pronounced hand-eye co-ordination problem. The child was unable to put any kind of puzzle together.

Barbara Vitale put the puzzle together for the child piece by piece, then got him to remove pieces and put them back straight away again in the same place. She then took all the pieces apart and muddled them up — and the child was suddenly able to put the puzzle together without any difficulty. Why?

Not only because she had previously shown him what the complete picture looked like — although this also helped — but also because she had shown him step-by-step how a puzzle is put together with its separate parts or taken apart again. She thus gave the child a tactile experience of the activity of puzzle-making, not only showing him the goal but also the procedure for accomplishing it.

In Ronald Davis's symbol mastery method, too, one learns through individual experience: the image-less 'trigger word' acquires a pictorial explanation — not as abstract definition but as self-created object. The dyslexic acquires a 'complete picture' relating to the word image, which he then incorporates into his thinking process. Through the subconscious mental image the word can then be mastered and no longer triggers confusion or disorientation. [92]

The child with disrupted hand-eye co-ordination had probably repeatedly activated his disorientation function. When he was subsequently able to develop a clear picture of the activity of puzzle-making, he no longer needed to do this.

From this and other examples it became clear to me how my six-year-old daughter learned to swim in such a strange way. Despite being unable to swim after attending a swimming course, she told me one day that she had decided to take her swimming badge 'the day after tomorrow.' When I asked her whether she had practised enough to do this, she told me that she had now sat long enough by the edge of the pool watching others learn to swim. And indeed, the day after next she gained her swimming badge without any difficulty, as if she had never done anything other than swim. By observing she had acquired a complete picture and could therefore now co-ordinate her movements precisely.

Below I will consider specific educational suggestions by Rudolf Steiner from the perspective of brain research, and assign them to corresponding hemisphere areas (L mode/R mode — the classification according to Meister Vitale and Edwards, p. 66 and 67).

Gerhard Huhn has also attempted something similar, by assigning teaching guidelines and curricula for the subject of textile design to the left-right schema, and thereby discovering the anomaly that, despite being primarily a craft subject for which right-hemisphere abilities are needed, it is taught in a predominantly left-dominant way.

I will continue to consider only the processes of reading, writing and engagement with language in general — and thus a discipline that does not primarily emphasize handwork skills. By its very nature, therefore, this area of learning would be assigned to the left hemisphere. Nevertheless we have seen from Vera Birkenbihl that learning functions best (i.e. is most brain friendly) where both hemispheres, or rather all brain capacities, are called upon simultaneously. I prefer to say 'all brain capacities' since it does not matter greatly which part of the brain localizes which 'areas of responsibility.' This may vary from person to person. The schematic division into L mode and R mode serves only as a simplified model to represent fundamentally different brain capacities and modes of perception, with the aim of considering all equally and linking them with each other as effectively as possible.

One thing at least has become crystal clear to me: brain-friendly learning is suitable for enabling not only right-hemisphere thinkers, but for all children to integrate their entire potential. Only then will we fulfil the need for children to develop freely, as Huhn and Birkenbihl call it; or, as Steiner formulated it ('full potential', see p. 45), the need to develop the human being's innate capacities.

Helping children to learn in a brain-friendly way is not therapy! Brain-friendly learning is an opportunity for all who learn. And 'brain-friendly' teaching is a challenge to all teachers.

Part III

...And now for some kind of connecting bridge

Learning Literacy

Rudolf Steiner made specific educational suggestions in relation to certain important areas of learning. Here are some examples:

The first day at school

In Steiner's works there are numerous references to the damaging effects on a child's free development if reading and writing are imposed on him too early. I have already referred frequently to his positive view of learning to read and write late. He regards the child's 'life of imagination' and not the 'life of reason' as the basis of education.[93]

Here, in my view, we can find a direct parallel with the L mode (life of reason) and R mode (life of imagination) classification. Steiner's often-expressed demand that we should always proceed 'from the whole' also corresponds to the R mode. His view about the connection between the way reading and writing are taught and the child's development has received highly topical (if perhaps unintentional) support. In the leaflet accompanying the game *Mega Memo* one reads:

Yet imagination and the ability to think pictorially contribute decisively to enhancing our memory and concentration. The present memory training game is based on insight into the fact that our photographic memory is most developed in childhood. Children do not think in abstractions but chiefly in images.

When is this capacity to think pictorially lost? When we learn the alphabet and literacy skills. The more our thinking is directed towards the meaning of letters, words and sentences, the more our pictorial thinking capacity fades into the background. (Haussmann/Geiselhart).

But just like us, Rudolf Steiner found himself compelled by the state to have literacy skills taught to children at his Waldorf School from Class One onwards (age six/seven). Since letters in their present form (L mode abstract symbol) are coupled with speech sounds and not pictures, he sought ways to render them comprehensible to children's imaginative life (R mode).

Let us examine his comments relating to the first lesson on the first day of school. On August 25, 1919, Steiner gave detailed suggestions for this first lesson, saying that 'In a certain respect this first lesson will have a more important, more far-reaching effect than all other lessons.'[94]

The most important thing for him initially is to explain to the children (= communication in speech / L mode) why they are here at school:

And you are here so that one day you too will be able to do what the big children can do (= invoking a picture, giving a sense of the whole / R mode).

It is striking how seriously and comprehensively he speaks here, perhaps for the time being talking over the children's heads, and outlining in advance all the details of what they will one day learn:

You see, the grown-ups have books and can read. You can't read yet but you will learn to; and once you have learned to read you will one day take up the books the grown-ups read, and find there all that the grown-ups know from them.

In the same way he goes on to explain writing, for instance that you can write letters and make notes about something, like the grown-ups; and maths, so that you can do everything right when you go shopping (giving a complete idea, proceeding from the whole / R mode).

It is of great importance for him that learning goals are brought clearly to children's awareness, and taken up respectfully by them. Such a method gives the children clarity and the best sense of orientation. This approach takes the child seriously: he doesn't just hear what he is to learn but also why: the reasons and the goals. In this way he is motivated and acquires a holistic overview.

Compare this with Ronald Davis's suggestions for counselling dyslexics: 'I will now sketch you an exact picture of what we are going to do, so that you know what's coming.'

Such a procedure testifies to deep respect for the other, something which unfortunately is often disregarded in diagnosis and therapy sessions; for instance by getting them to repeat nonsense words, carry out random movement sequences or draw certain motifs without telling them why.

Children who have the disorientation gift will automatically use this brain function to seek sense in the set task. They inevitably become confused, and diagnosis or therapy results are distorted. In the worst case, trust in and respect for the adult is damaged, even if children do not sense this rationally but only emotionally to begin with. They feel they're being messed about or made a fool of.

For Rudolf Steiner, at any rate, an 'appropriate' clarification of the goal of learning belongs intrinsically to the conditions for successful learning.

After speaking in an appropriate way, as I've described — which is intended to help the child become aware of why he is there in school, on the one hand, and on the other can give the child a certain regard and respect for the adult — it is important to pass on to something else.

It is good, for example, to say: 'Now take a look at yourselves. You have two hands, a left and a right. These hands enable you to work — you can do all sorts of things with them.' In other words you also try to make the children aware of what human beings possess. The child should not just know instinctively that he has hands but also become aware of this.

Of course you may say that the child is already aware of having hands. Yet there is a difference between knowing he has hands for working, or whether this thought has never passed through his soul.

After speaking with the children for a while about working with their hands, the next step is to get them to actually use this facility. This could possibly happen in the very first lesson. You can say: 'I am going to do this (Steiner draws a vertical line on the board). Now each of you can do the same with your hand.'

You can get the children to do the same, as slowly as possible; it will take quite a while if you call the children out one by one and get them to do this on the board. Proper absorption of the lesson is of the greatest importance here.

Afterwards you can tell the children: 'Now I will do this (draws a curved line on the board); now use your hand to do this as well.' And each child again does this.

After doing this you can say to them: 'This is a straight line, and the other is a curved line.' So you have now used your hands to draw a straight and a curved line.' You can help the children who are less skilled, but ensure that each one completes the task properly from the outset. In this way you make sure you get the children to do something from the first moment, and then ensure that this is repeated in subsequent lessons. In the next lesson, therefore, get them to do a straight and a curved line once more.

Now a subtle aspect needs to be considered here. You don't yet need to place any great value on getting the children to draw a straight and a curved line from memory; but instead, the next time, draw a straight line on the board again, get the children to imitate it, and likewise the curved line; and now turn to one child and ask: 'What is that?' 'A straight line!' And turn to another, and ask: 'And what is this?' 'A curved line!'

In other words you should use the principle of repetition by getting the child to repeat the drawing and then, rather than you telling them, getting them to say what they have done. It is very important to use this subtle nuance.

In general you need to place great value on doing and repeating things properly in the children's presence so that the lessons you teach can become habitual for them. [95]

Here we see that in relation to the first specific 'work' at school, Rudolf Steiner first explains in detail (= speech / L mode) what is needed in order to carry out this work: first he wants the children to be aware of how their hands can be used and the work they can accomplish, before getting each child to realize this through imitation (= starting from the whole, leading to tangible, haptic experience / R mode).

For Steiner, learning is not some kind of quiz event, giving worth to those children who can already do something, while exposing those who can't. He first presents the expected result, giving a clear example for them to imitate: he draws the straight line and the curved line on the board and only after the children have successfully copied him, and acquired their own tactile experience, does he give the lines their name: a straight line and a curved line.

In this way they learn the abstract shapes of a line: only after the experience has become tangible for each, is it given a name.

By getting the children to acquire their own experience, Steiner adds to the abstract symbol (= L mode) the missing right-hemisphere element (= R mode), thus bringing the abstract within 'grasp' — a word whose literal and pictorial meaning conceals an ancient wisdom of teaching.

In following lessons this process is repeated. Again, after completing the work (= R mode), the child is to name the form himself: a straight line, a curved line (= L mode). Slowly, holistic understanding is engendered: how something looks (= picture) and what it is called (= language).

Compare this with Ronald Davis's suggestions for counselling work with dyslexics: 'Familiarize students with clay. Shaping. Cutting. Rolling.' (This is before shaping the letters of the alphabet.) Often the student first has to be shown that he needs straight and curved clay rolls in order to form the letters. Once a clear example has been provided, the dyslexic finds it easy to co-ordinate eye and hand in the right way. This is also how Steiner went about teaching the straight and curved line.

Being able to complete such lines consciously is important for carrying out many school activities, such as writing, maths symbols, geometry etc. Lack of clarity when learning to make lines and shapes can mean that children with a dyslexic tendency become confused, thus triggering disorientation. This can become apparent in massive handwriting problems. [96]

The importance of giving a clear example was brought home to me recently in my own advisory work with a ten-year-old dyslexic student. I showed her how to work the clay to produce the alphabet, which was no problem for her. But when we were going to move on to practise symbol mastery with words, something entirely unexpected occurred: she refused, saying she could not form any 'figures' or other modelled shapes. She had never modelled in her life, she said (although this wasn't strictly true; but she had probably never fully experienced how a three-dimensional shape is formed).

In our next session I got her to model a sphere and a cube, the models for which lay physically on the table in front of her. I also showed her how one can compose figures from clay rolls and a sphere, and got her to do this. In the following session, when we were again going to try to make a symbol model, she no longer had any problem (in fact it was almost incredible how easy she found it) in modelling a guinea pig, a cat, a man, a letter, a porch etc.

For Barbara Meister Vitale, too, example models, complete concepts and clear objectives are of the greatest importance:

As I have mentioned many times, right-brained children often are visual learners. They may need to see a picture of the completed task before they can visualize what they are to do. Teachers and parents may provide this support in the following ways:

1. When asking a child to complete a structured craft activity, provide a completed sample for him.

2. When asking the child to practise the mastery of a new concept, do an example for him.

3. Do the first problem on a maths paper or reading ditto. [97]

Her choice of teaching method also shows an interesting connection with Rudolf Steiner's 'first lesson':

There are children who learn beautifully standing up ... Right-hemispheric children seem to be movers ... I urge you to try this in your own classroom the next time you teach an arithmetic lesson. Put your so-called right-hemispheric children at the chalkboard doing problems while your left-hemispheric children are in their seats working the same problems on paper. [98]

In summary, I find in Steiner's remarks about the first lesson at school an optimum, brain-friendly means for conveying and teaching abstract symbols (straight and curved lines). Abstract things can be mastered, and at the same time the children familiarize themselves with a 'tool' they will need in future: consciously performed hand skills.

This consciousness is indeed of great importance, for the right-hemisphere child, who:

... displays fine motor problems (cutting, writing or pasting) when asked to conform or do structured tasks. Fine motor problems rarely appear when the child is doing something he has selected. [99]

The fact that many former Waldorf pupils recall the 'straight line and curve' lesson when they're adults, shows that they mastered these symbols as concepts.

In my view, however, there is a serious disparity here between Steiner's intentions and the practice at Waldorf schools: Rudolf Steiner had no wish to create symbols for 'straight' and 'curved.' In fact he never used these terms in isolation. He was in no way concerned to specifically convey the vertical or a semi-circle open to the right, as these are seen on the board drawing illustrated on page 97. While he certainly (either intentionally or intuitively) chose these archetypal forms, his aim was to awaken a very general sense and understanding of various abstract lines (= L mode) and enable the children to draw them.

One has to re-read his words very carefully:

'A straight line' is something quite different from the concept 'the straight line' and 'a curved line' is not at all the same as 'the curve.' The indefinite article 'a' is, precisely, indefinite, while the definite article 'the' refers to something specific. In the phrase 'the straight line' its quality becomes substantive, fixed as noun. 'A line' likewise has substance but its properties can alter, can become either straight or curved (see Steiner's remarks on different parts of speech, p. 142f).

A line can be transposed to other lines and allows the possibility of further analogous transformation (= R mode); the concept 'the straight line' is fixed, on the other hand, and, without a further process of abstraction, can only be applied to the specifically learned straight line.

Can you sense the difference?

I only became aware of the difference in significance myself when helping pupils to gain symbol mastery of the so-called trigger words. A thirteen-year-old dyslexic explained the indefinite article 'a' as something which still contains a question or lack of definition and clarity. She got the idea for a scene that would show me what she meant:

In Antoine de Saint-Exupéry's novella, *The Little Prince*, the little prince asks the narrator to 'Draw me *a* sheep!' But the narrator doesn't know how to draw a sheep, so his attempts to do so fail. For communication to work, more information is needed: an example or model (both already know what 'sheep' looks like) and if necessary the determination of certain properties (= straight or curved line, and the little prince's objections about what properties a sheep must not have). 'Draw me *the* sheep!' on the other hand, would be fully determined and defined; and the little prince would not have wished this. Thus a hidden sheep in a box corresponded precisely to the meaning of 'a'.

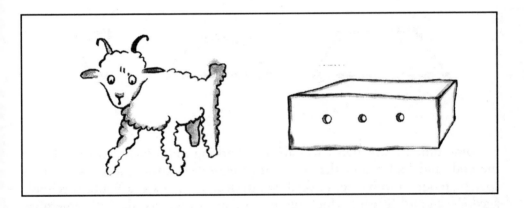

I am still in the process of learning to attend precisely to subtle nuances or to express myself in a clearly differentiated way. There's still a long way to go, but Rudolf Steiner invites me, and all of us, to pursue this path when he says:

People today are terribly sloppy inwardly. When they listen to something they do very bad inward eurythmy ... Sometimes they express this naively, for instance by asserting: 'Dr. Steiner says many fine things, but he says nothing new!' People have become so rigid in their listening that they haze over everything except the habits of thought that have rigidified in them over decades. Unless people's listening is re-awoken by eurythmy, they will remain unable to listen in our age, and will grow ever less able to do so.[100]

In urging us to make language visible again (in eurythmy) he hopes to meet with better understanding. I have often experienced how pictorial thinkers complain about my 'hazy' language, because I fail to notice fine nuances.[101]

From picture to letter

I have repeatedly wondered what is so different in the way Rudolf Steiner introduces letters from ordinary methods of teaching literacy. And at the same time I keep asking myself why his method is no more accessible for dyslexics. The stories and pictures used to introduce letters in Waldorf schools ought surely to be very well suited to the particular mode of thinking of these pictorial thinkers.

I myself found the roof (German = *Dach*) that is turned on its side and becomes the letter D confusing, and thought this could lead children to reverse the letter; but my 'logical' train of thought got me nowhere.

Some time back, when I was already working intensively with the Davis method, and had found that dyslexics themselves know most about their specific mode of thinking, I asked two dyslexics (pupils at a Waldorf school, aged eleven and fifteen) which pictures or stories they could still remember from the lessons introducing letters.

To my surprise, they mentioned the D and its changed position: 'There was a roof (Dach) which turned into a D.' A table shape became a T. Water came out of a round hole in the mountains, and this was the Q of '*Quelle*' (spring). The M was initially as rounded as 'the M in McDonald's'; in their main lesson book*. I found an upper lip that later became the letter M.[102]

They also explained that the letter 'I' was a tree trunk, but then they retracted this, saying it wasn't so because the 'I' and the tree trunk only share the same shape (there is no sound relationship).

These pupils had no memory of the stories and tales used to introduce the letters, but only of the letters with which they connected certain shapes.

When I looked at their old main lesson books, I was surprised that they mentioned letters which they had only illustrated fleetingly: the upended D of the roof (without a house) and the single upper lip (without a face) etc.

---

*   In Waldorf schools, the main lesson is the first period of about two hours each morning, when particular subjects are dealt with at length for three or four weeks at a time.

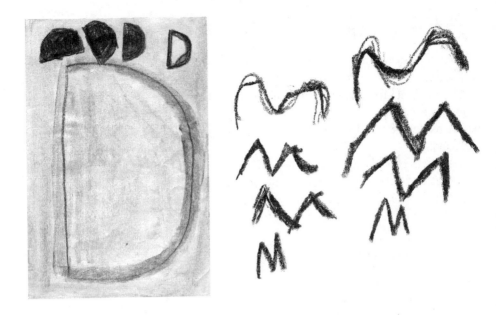

Ronja, class 1 (aged 6/7)

At the time I simply took note of this and wrote it down, because I couldn't understand it, until I found an exercise by Vera Birkenbihl in the leaflet accompanying her brain-training game. Suddenly I found the answer and began to grasp why these pupils could retain these particular letters so well.

So you can get a hands-on sense of what I discovered, I'll invite you to do this exercise yourself. Vera Birkenbihl writes:[*]

Writing secret scripts is a wonderful way to train the right half of the brain, provided you write them by hand. Do you want to have a go?

Take a piece of paper and a pencil, and 'translate' your name and your address into the code given overleaf. Good. Now translate the following sentence into it too:

Seeing means touching with the eyes. [**]

Now shut this book: which letter pairings do you still recall? Note these down before you read any further.

---

[*] This won't work as well in the English translation due to language differences, but for many of the letters of the alphabet it is still appropriate.

[**] Steiner: 'What one calls 'seeing' in modern parlance is in reality just a more complex form of touching. (Steiner, GA 206, lecture 15: 23 July, 1921)

A =   O =

B =   P =

C =   Q =

D =   R =

E =   S =

F =   T =

G =   U =

H =   V =

I =   W =

J =   X =

K =   Y =

L =   Z =

M =   CH =

N =   SCH =

How many could you remember? None, six or more than twelve? Did you enjoy doing this exercise? Was it difficult for you? Please note these findings.

Now turn over to page 106 and see which symbols are assigned to which letters.

Before you go on reading, please shut the book again, take a new sheet of paper and write down all the paired letters/symbols which you can now recall!

That's how effective brain-friendly processes are! Apparently entirely abstract signs can be recalled very well the moment we connect a pictorial idea with them.

If you compare your first test result with the second, how do you feel now? Did it motivate, excite, astonish or even amuse you to discover the principle upon which our original code was based?

Whether the pictorial connections are already inherent in the symbol (as in this secret script) or whether you yourself first have to create a pictorial connection (picture sequences, peg technique, mnemonics etc.) images always make things easier!

As with Steiner, each letter is derived from the shape of an object depicted by a word starting with that letter. Yet how neutrally and soberly the 'Birkenbihl alphabet' is presented: no stories or fairy tales cluster round each picture, such as are usually used to introduce each letter in Waldorf schools. [103]

Unlike Waldorf main lesson books, whole words are not given following the initial letter, nor are additional words starting with that letter given (e.g. after Mouth, come Man, Milk, Moon etc.). Why?

Where and why did Rudolf Steiner package the introduction to letters in so much padding? Despite having already read everything by him that I could find on this theme, I once again leafed through his comments on literacy teaching and, to my surprise, found that he never did!

Just like Vera Birkenbihl, he simply took objects from daily life that are suited to depicting the shape of a letter. (Steiner restricts himself here to the consonants, and develops the vowels in a different way.) He mentions neither imaginative stories in which the things or animals he uses are embedded, nor does he go on to give a whole word that starts with that letter (e.g. *Dach* [roof] or *Mund* [mouth]). He simply connects the shape with the sound. Often, also, he draws several steps to show how, for instance, the F gradually develops from the shape of a fish.[104]

A = Eye (Auge) = =

B = Picture (Bild) = =

C = C note = =

D = Domino = =

E = Rings (Ehringe) := =

F = Fish = =

G = Fork (Gabel) = =

H = Hand = =

I = Hedgehog (Igel) = =

J = Jesus = =

K = Suitcase (Koffer) = =

L = Love (Leibe) = =

M = Moon (Mond) = =

N = Needle (Nadel) = =

O = Ear (Ohr) =

P = Planet =

Q = Square (Quadrant) =

R = Roundabout =

S = Sun (Sonne) =

T = Tennis =

U = Clock (Uhr) =

V = Bird (Vogel) =

W = World (Welt) =

X = x axis =

Y = y axis =

Z = Zeppelin =

CH = Chinaman =

SH = Ship (Schiff) =

Elsewhere, he even develops the fish from a reversed or reflected fish. [105]

No doubt there are reasons for using so many 'pictorial' additions in modern Waldorf literacy practice, but it must be permissible to ponder why Steiner himself seems to have dispensed with this.

Even his basic stance differs from that of all other literacy theorists when he says that learning to read and write around the age of seven is something 'quite alien to human nature.' [106]

He justifies his view by saying that our script is based on conventions that have been developed by human beings on what he calls the 'physical plane:'

When we teach children to read and write we are teaching in the most physical realm of all; less so when we teach them maths; and when we teach children music, drawing and suchlike we are really teaching the soul-spirit or the spirit-soul. [107]

In this context an interesting parallel to the findings of brain research occurs to me: writing, reading and speech sounds are centred in the left hemisphere; maths occupies both hemispheres, subdivided into 'simple numeracy' (L mode) and 'mathematical numeracy' (R mode); and everything of an artistic nature falls under the capacities of the right hemisphere.

There's something else: whereas I was struck by the marked ambidexterity of the Egyptians, as I mentioned, Steiner states that we lack the 'Egyptian element' in our script:

Just recall that the ancient Egyptians still had a pictorial script, pictograms. The images they fixed as script still retained a similarity with what they indicated.

This pictorial script still had a certain intrinsic meaning — even cuneiform writing had a certain meaning too, although this tended to express more of a will element, whereas pictograms expressed more of a feeling and thinking element. In both these ancient forms of writing, when people read them, they could be aware that there was still some connection with what surrounded them in the outer world.

But these squiggles on the board have nothing to do with 'father', yet it is with such marks that the child is now supposed to get to grips. It's no wonder if he refuses to. [108]

Nevertheless, to accommodate official requirements, Steiner tries to connect the Egyptians' pictorial script with today's phonetic script:

One doesn't after all educate children for themselves only, but for life; they have to learn to read and write. The question is merely how one should teach them in a way that does not contradict human nature. [109]

In hieroglyphs the whole word appears as an image symbol. The fish drawing is identical with the meaning 'fish.' This is not altered if one depicts the symbol in reverse. This is why the shape of a roof turned on its side does not lead to confusion, but corresponds rather to the 'nature' of human thinking. [110]

The pure pictograms did in fact later become phonetic signs for the Egyptians too, but these could still be related back to the original pictograms. Hebrew letters, also, are derived from a picture symbol. To make similar kinds of connection, Rudolf Steiner tried to find everyday things from whose shape the initial letter of the word designating them could be derived.

From this you can see how one derives the letter from the picture, and can in turn draw the picture from life itself ... In the case of the consonants you will always find something which allows you to start from things themselves. [111]

You will always take pleasure, even if in a very subdued sense, when you transfer to letters the shape you yourself have discovered of some animal or plant ... so that the initial letter of a word is a drawing for the shape of an animal or plant, or also for any external object ... [112]

In other words, one derives from life itself what initially can be present as drawing, and then one transposes it into the shapes of the letters. [113]

The point here is ... to lead on from an object, from life itself, into the shapes of letters. Here you will have every opportunity to derive letter shapes for the child from external reality. [114]

Steiner places value on deriving the images used from the children's reality and — in complete contrast to stories of fairy tales about third persons — he personally addresses each child's individual range of experience. In other words, the child in included and 'in the picture.' Our expression 'being in the picture' or 'putting someone in the picture' is a fairly accurate expression for the way in which one can gain access and mastery by this means.

It is interesting to see the importance of this inclusion of the child in what is taught in Davis's work with symbol mastery. For children with attention deficit disorders (ADD) it is recommended that the ego-self of the child should always be invoked and involved in developing abstract concepts, for instance the word 'consequence':

> *Whenever a fundamental concept is to be mastered, the clay model must show the individual in relation to the basic concept. This is what makes the difference between something learned and a concept that becomes a part of this person's identity.* [115]

This makes sense of another instruction from the Davis method; after the student has modelled the alphabet, one asks

> *... the student, 'Whose alphabet is this?' Repeat the question conversationally until the student says, 'It's mine.' Then ask the student, 'Why?' or 'How come?' until the student says 'Because I made it,' or 'Because I created it.'* [116]

In other words, we learn and retain things better if we include ourselves in the process. Rudolf Steiner once described this very tangibly:

> *Let's imagine we place a safety pin on the edge of a table, on its corner, and as we do so form a clear image of the right-angle of the table with the safety pin positioned between the table's two edges. Then we leave it there confidently. If I only do this once it probably won't work, but if I make a habit of it, my forgetfulness will gradually improve. This exercise works because we form a very specific thought — that I'm placing the safety pin in a particular place and surroundings. By doing this I consciously connect my ego or 'I' with the action I take, and also form a clear picture. Picturing what I do as I think about it, connecting my 'I,' the essential core of my being, with a pictorial image, sharpens the memory greatly. Such an exercise can be of practical benefit by making us less forgetful.*
> *This kind of exercise, however, can also achieve a great deal more ... this simple habit will increasingly strengthen the etheric body.* [117]

Based on this insight he also makes use of the I or ego when it comes to introducing letters. He does not say 'Once upon a time there was a fish,' but:

> *'You've seen a fish, haven't you? Remember for a moment what it looked like, the fish you saw (= imagining/thinking!). Now I'm going to draw this, which looks very similar to a fish. The fish you saw pretty much resembles what you can see on the board now. Now think about how you say the word "fish" (= imagining/thinking!)*

What you say when you say 'fish' is contained in this sign (see left drawing on p.105). Now try, instead of saying the whole word "fish," just to say the beginning of it ... And now one tries to show the child that he need only say the beginning of the word "fish" (= language!): F - f - f - f.

And now you've started to say the word "fish." And now just think that people gradually found a way of making what you see there simpler (see right drawing on p. 105). When you start saying the word "fish" (= language!), F - f - f - f, you can express this, when you write it down, by making this sign. And this sign is what people call "f."

So now you have learned that what you say when you speak the word "fish" begins with "f" — and now you write that down as "f." When you start writing the word "fish" you always breathe like this, F - f - f - f. So you are learning to recognize the sign that starts the word you speak for fish.' [118]

As with Davis's symbol mastery, image, purpose and language here occur simultaneously: the letter F looks like this, it represents a sign for a certain initial speech sound, and it sounds like F - f - f .

Steiner uses a lot of words to get from the fish to F, but not once does he depart from reality, either in word or thought. The child is to simply picture a fish from his own experience, not one drawn from the tale of *The Fisherman and his Wife* or some other context. Nor is this derived from a story about a third person. If one were to take a fairy tale or suchlike in order to arrive at the letter form, there might be a danger that children — at least the right-hemisphere ones — might take flight into the 'world of unicorns.'

Sunk in the fantastic realm of their right hemisphere, they would only gain a distorted perception of the reality: a letter could be taken in a 'wrong' (= disorientated) way, or not absorbed at all. This is why Steiner does not derive the W from 'witch,' the G from 'giant,' the D from 'dragon' or the P from 'pixie.'

Those who object that Steiner's example for the letter B is derived from the picture of a bear, and therefore might be associated with *Snow White and Rose Red* or another fairy tale, should consider that dancing bears in market places were still part of children's immediate experience at the beginning of the twentieth century. Steiner himself refers to such a dancing bear. [119]

I will return later to Steiner's educational suggestions in relation to texts, for I think that he was very aware of the danger of disorientation.

But why, in all his preserved board drawings on introducing the letters, does he not proceed to a whole word? Why does he stay with the F without showing the whole word 'fish?'

I believe there is only one explanation: that he thought this would be confusing, for there is nothing of the fish in the other letters. Is the F connected with the fish, or is it instead, or also, contained with the I, the S or the H? Confusion leads to disorientation, which must be avoided when teaching letters.

As a further means of introducing the consonants, Steiner mentions developing and drawing the letter L from the movement of a leg walking (*laufen* in German), or the S from the wind's blowing (*sausen* = sighing, soughing). [120]

This likewise corresponds to a brain-friendly procedure: he connects spatial awareness (= R mode) to the initial sounds (= L mode) for walking (*laufen*) and blowing (*sausen*).

He does the same when it comes to introducing vowels: drawing on the children's world of feeling (= R mode) he expresses emotions in gestures, represents these as a drawing or sketch, and thus leads them into the shape of a letter.

Once again, he starts from what each child is familiar with, and includes each child personally in the picture:

'Now imagine the sun which you see rising each morning. Can any of you remember what you do as you see the sun rising in the morning?'

One or another child may perhaps recall what he does. If none remember, you have to help the child a little to remember what he does, how he stands, what he will have said if he saw a lovely sunrise: 'Ah!'

You have to summon this kind of feeling, and try to draw from it the resonance that sounds in the vowel.

And then you have to try to say something like: 'If you stand like this and say "Ah!" it is as if two sunbeams stream out of you from within, through your mouth, and go further and further apart.

What lives inside you when you see the sunrise, you let it stream out of you like this (see left-hand picture) when you say "Ah".*

However, you do not let it stream out of you completely, but you keep some of it back, and so it becomes this sign (see right-hand picture).'

You can try to draw the nature of the vowel, to clothe it in pictorial form. By doing so you get drawings which can pictorially represent how the signs for the vowels arose. [121]

---

*   In German the letter 'A' sounds like 'Ah.'

Here I'd like to return for a moment to Steiner's introduction of the letter F, and accentuate one thing in particular which he says: 'And this sign is what people call F.'

Something abstract for the children — yet now brought closer to them through the picture of the fish — is now given a name. Even if it appears more 'logical' to us to familiarize children only with the phonetic sounds of letters initially (= step-by-step procedure / L mode), Steiner calls the letters by their proper name from the outset and does not just continue saying the sound (F - f - f - f).

I know that this is at odds with current practice, especially in mainstream schools, where parents are often urged to refer to the letters by their phonetic sounds only, but let us examine this from the perspective of the R mode for a moment. A sound, F - f - f - f, in reality has no correspondence in speech: there are no 'proper' words that consist only of a single consonant.

But to master and possess something, this 'something' needs a specific name.

Whatever or whoever has a name exists fully, and can be recalled. This awareness is clearly deeply rooted in us — whether you look at the Bible ('I have called thee by thy name; thou art mine') or a book of fairy tales ('Today I bake, tomorrow brew, the next I'll have the young queen's child. Ha, glad am I that no one knew that Rumpelstiltskin I am styled.') And should this not be true, likewise, of letters?

Perhaps precisely because it is illogical (= R mode) it is important for holistic understanding, as the precondition for successful learning, that children also know a letter's name from the very outset. [122]

In introducing the letters, therefore, Rudolf Steiner starts from children's own experience: in things, movements, or in the world of feeling he seeks a connection with abstract symbols. But he does something else too: he expressly mentions rendering individual letters tangible by modelling them. From this I conclude that he would have nothing against modelling the whole alphabet, as Ronald Davis describes in his book. [123] In my view this could easily be incorporated into teaching in Waldorf schools, and elsewhere. It could come at the end of the lessons to introduce letters, and then be used again later to introduce the lower case alphabet (in Waldorf schools, unlike mainstream primary schools, the capitals are introduced first). The alphabet as a whole, the naming of its parts, and the significance of individual letters within the alphabet, all give orientation. The letters become accessible and graspable, acquiring value as parts of a whole. Such symbol mastery of the alphabet, in my view at least, receives outstanding affirmation in Steiner's suggestion that: 'The alphabet is an expression of the secret of the human being.' [124]

If one decides to get children to model the whole alphabet, the question arises as to the most suitable material for this. Possibilities include clay, wax, plasticine or something similar — maybe even mud or 'dirt from the street' as Steiner once contemplated. [125]

I'd like to give some advice here: colourless, re-useable, easily worked and also cheap plasticine has proven best in my own experience.

To maintain the wholeness and clarity of the alphabet from the beginning, it is important that children see the whole alphabet, in both upper and lower cases, depicted in the classroom from the moment they start working on the letters. This 'example' or model is particularly important nowadays since we are confronted on every street corner by so many different fonts and letter shapes (e.g. brand names and logos). There is therefore a danger that whole words or terms can be understood as fixed symbols, rather than being seen as composed of separate parts (*see* 'wish list' on p.20 LEGO).

From sentence to word to letter to sound

Besides the procedure just described, Rudolf Steiner recommends another way of learning the constituents of written language. I suspect that these suggestions have led to the confusion between Steiner's original thoughts and the method used in Waldorf schools for introducing letters through their shapes. For example, this has given rise to words as end product, for in a linear way of thinking it appears to us logical (= L mode), after learning the letter F, to proceed immediately to other words starting with F, such as floor, flea or face ...

Yet Rudolf Steiner works in a holistic, rather than linear way:

Then one continues by drawing the child's attention to the fact that the letter he has seen at the beginning of a word also occurs in the middle of a word. So one can say to the child: * *'You know the bright yellow flower that grows in spring [= picture / R mode + direct address = being in the picture oneself], which some people pick and put in bunches indoors: the daffodil [= language designation / L mode]. Grown-ups write "daffodil" like this [= i.e. it is just a convention, and has nothing intrinsically to do with the daffodil]: DAFFODIL. Now just see, if you say this very slowly [= one has to imagine 'saying' or 'speaking' if one does not automatically speak the word inwardly when thinking / R and L mode]: Daffodil. In the middle you find the same thing that was at the beginning of "fish."' You always write it in large letters first, so that the child can see the similarity of the image [= no use of a confusingly different font or text image / analogy / R and L mode].* [126]

Although I long since marked this passage for myself as 'outstanding' I only just became aware of the genius in it as I was writing it out. In this way Steiner shows how we can proceed from a whole word to a letter.

---

*   Steiner has a different example, using the letter 'B': the German word for 'vine' — Rebe

You can find further examples of this in the same passage (and in GA 301, lecture 10: May 5, 1920). The path from sentence to word and thence to the letter can also be pursued (*see* both of the above lectures).

The parallel is unmistakeable. In the book by Hermann Ehmann that I have referred to several times, *Is my child dyslexic?* (unavailable in English) the author criticizes traditional therapy approaches. In examining the various learning techniques, he arrives at the following conclusion:

I am unable here to give a summary of the best techniques for learning or memorizing. But I'd like to cite one of the most effective and most frequently used learning aids, the technique of visualization. This is a very ancient method of imagining things pictorially that originally derives from the domain of mysticism or religion. It is very well suited to supporting good literacy skills ...

The visualization exercise is like this: the child shuts his eyes and simply imagines a cat [= picturing] — one he may already know [= taken from direct experience]: her colour, silky fur, how she lounges on the ground, how she cleans herself, catches a mouse, or whatever else the child imagines [= complete picture/concept]. If the child now remembers this picture he will never again forget the word 'cat,' as long as he has once seen it properly written [= simultaneity with the word picture].[127]

U.A.F.S.

Filine, aged 13

In the case of Davis's method of symbol mastery, too, the dyslexic is asked, after making his model, to form a complete picture/concept of it, and the text image that belongs to it. Something that has proven particularly effective is to recite the letters backwards, as if 'reading them off' an imaginary wall. Learning and memory techniques such as the visualization technique or reverse sequence review can also be found frequently amongst Rudolf Steiner's thought exercises for adults, especially in his lecture of January 18, 1909: 'Practical Training in Thought'.[128]

The path from the word to the letter, and even from the sentence to the word to the letter, as advocated by Steiner, corresponds to the analytic or whole-word method used in teaching literacy:

That is why, in the Waldorf School, we don't teach by starting from the letters and developing a synthesis from there, but rather we begin with the complete sentence, analysing out the words within it, then take the words and derive or analyse the letters out of them, and then find the sounds for the letters. By this means we get the children to internalize things in the right way. [129]

Ricarda, aged 11

One can cite many arguments from debate over recent decades in relation to the 'whole-word method, and/or the 'synthetic method'. Literacy experts have said a great deal about this.

In his article 'Were the pharaohs dyslexic?' A. Kaulins reports on a teacher in America who taught basic reading and writing for over forty years with the whole-word method, and only later progressed to phonetics once the pupils knew how to read and write. [130] She never had any dyslexics in her class.

In contrast to this, current views consider it advisable to teach both methods at once, and this has also found its way into Waldorf education, as witnessed by the following extract from a pamphlet publicizing Waldorf education in Germany:

Alongside introducing individual letters pictorially, and from there passing on to developing words synthetically, the reverse, analytic path should be practised equally intensively ...

The synthetic mode, in which words are derived from constituent letters, reduces the risk of dyslexia ...

This, it seems very clear to me, is a misconception based on our predominantly verbal and linear thinking.

The whole-word method in foreign-language teaching

In my view, an excellent way of using the whole-word method in foreign-language teaching* is offered by the Ladybird Key Word Reading Scheme used in England. Coupled with orientation and symbol mastery as taught by Davis, I have found this to be a good means of helping even children with pronounced dyslexia to make a good deal of progress in mastering English as a foreign language. The scheme is a programme from the seventies for teaching literacy to English children. In twelve sections, each consisting of three small volumes, simple texts drawn from children's immediate experience (though now somewhat out of date) develop a vocabulary enhanced by brain-friendly pictures.

In the first eight units, the 300 most commonly used words of the English language are learned, the so-called 'key words.' Almost all of these are also on the list of English trigger words .[131] The reason for learning these key words is that they compose three-quarters of normal texts for children and teenagers.

H. J. Modlmayr developed this concept for use in foreign-language teaching. He uses these books for teaching English at secondary schools, following which he embarks on works such as J.R.R Tolkien's *The Hobbit* as early as the age of 13/14. [132]

---

* This passage is of course presented from the viewpoint of German pupils.

However, in my view the whole-word method definitely has to take account of the pictorial nature of a word in order to be understood by pictorial thinkers. (In relation to this, see the above passages by Steiner relating to the daffodil, and by Ehmann to the cat, as well as Davis on symbol mastery of trigger words.)

I found no justification by Steiner of learning literacy by synthetic means! This synthesis only occurs considerably later, after the analytic process has been grasped (*see* above).

Using fairy tales and stories

Rudolf Steiner places great value on telling children fairy tales, legends and stories from a young age, though not in connection with the introduction of literacy.

If one examines his educational suggestions more closely, one notices the differentiated way in which he recommends the use of musical and artistic elements in teaching. Precisely he, who recognized so clearly the fundamental value of music and art (=R mode) in child development, and repeatedly emphasized its importance, warns vehemently against arbitrarily muddling up the different goals of education.

Everything of an artistic nature — painting, craft work, music and likewise fairy-tale telling — has its own specific educational task and should not merely be used as a means to an end, for instance to 'create a mood' as the basis for something quite different to be developed.

When Steiner gets children, for instance, to paint a mouth in red, as a way of leading on to the letter M, allowing the children themselves to create the picture and then derive the letter from it, he remains consistently in the children's own world of immediate experience, thus establishing a direct connection between content and artistic expression.[133]

I am certain, in this context, that he would not have conceived the idea of drawing on the well-known sentence from *Little Red Riding Hood*, 'What a big mouth you have grandmother!' since there is no link here between the nature of the fairy tale and the educational goal of learning to write.

In the 'meetings with teachers' he is unusually clear about this:

What you have just said now is nonsense. You see, we mustn't introduce a custom which will, on the one hand, impair teaching through an artificially created mood; and on the other hand we shouldn't use art for such a purpose. Art must be allowed to remain a purpose sufficient to itself, not something used to prepare a mood. This seems to me worryingly close to spiritualist séances. I don't think that ought to be pursued ...

There is no connection between the Punic wars and music. What kind of connection could there be? What's the purpose of it? Nor should you use eurythmy here! It's certainly the case that you can't give a eurythmy performance in order to set the mood for a shadow construct.

Do you want to give a eurythmy performance as prelude to sending a waybill or bill of consignment? That would be taking things in the other direction. Our task is to make teaching as inwardly musical as possible, but not through purely outward means. That's harmful for the content of what is presented, and likewise for art itself.

One cannot tell a fairy tale in order, afterwards, to teach colour theory, for this would seriously lead teaching astray. The lessons must themselves be inwardly created in a way that engenders a certain mood.

If there's a need first of all to create a mood with some kind of externally decorative thing — which does injury to art itself — this would be tantamount to saying that one is unable or unwilling to create this mood through the content of teaching itself.

I always found it worrying when some piece of music was performed, sometimes, as a prelude to a talk on anthroposophy — although this isn't quite the same thing, since adults are involved. In the school curriculum this just isn't on. We'll have to get rid of it. [134]

Where, on the other hand, Rudolf Steiner does recommend using fairy tales and stories in lessons, this is always with a specific learning goal:

The first thing we should consider is that when we receive children in Class One, we need to find suitable story material for telling to them, and for getting them to repeat afterwards.

We develop their speech by telling them fairy tales, legends — but also externally realistic occurrences; and the same applies to getting them to recap what they've heard. Here we can develop a transition from the colloquial vernacular to more educated speech. By ensuring that the child speaks properly, we will be giving him the basis for writing properly too. [135]

The goal of telling fairy tales is therefore, initially, to get children to speak well, which Steiner regards as an indispensable basis for writing properly. Ordered thoughts, a differentiated choice of words, correct expression, clear sentence construction, good style, correct grammar — all this follows from attentive listening, matures into clear thought pictures, flowers in good speech through retelling of the story, and finally ripens as good and then also correctly spelled writing.

Let's just recall his complaint, in his *Autobiography*, at how he had such trouble in suddenly having to 'properly' write words he'd previously only heard in vernacular language (in his case, dialect).

Thus fairy tales and stories can and should achieve proper speech through listening, and proper writing through retelling. A very important use for them! But their use does not extend to introducing the letters, even if Steiner continues by saying, 'This telling and retelling of stories can run parallel to leading the child into a certain artistic language of forms,' after which he then mentions literacy development.

Yet he explicitly does not say, 'Thus we lead the children into a "certain artistic language of forms" and thence, by this means, to the letters;' instead he just recommends that these things can run parallel to or accompany each other. If I think of parallels in literal, pictorial terms, they only meet at infinity. In other words, Steiner is not yet advocating that these two areas of learning should be linked together.

I certainly don't want to suggest there is no place for storytelling in school — quite the opposite. The current trend is a generally observed impoverishment of spoken language (involving not only a reduced vocabulary and expressiveness but also poor grammar and syntax). This can be remedied and oral expression can be developed through close listening and detailed retelling. Whatever one's personal views about advances in technology and the media of today and tomorrow, the age of speech-recognition technology is upon us and, while no longer requiring perfect spelling, it does increasingly depend on the capacity to speak in a 'print-ready' fashion. (In this context, Barry Sanders's observations, in his book *A is for Ox: The Collapse of Literacy and the Rise of Violence in an Electronic Age,* accentuate the importance of acquiring good oral speech as the basis for later acquisition of written language, though I do not agree at all with his other views about 'orality' and literacy.)

Not until Class Two (age seven/eight) does Rudolf Steiner envisage getting the children to take the path from verbal to written retelling, to creative writing — and thus to use, rather than acquire, literacy skills. Alongside proper, intentional speech, a further reason for the continual practice of retelling, for Rudolf Steiner, is to gain a proper, conscious experience of reality: 'Recounting and retelling what has happened or been experienced should be nurtured in primary school far more than so-called "free writing."' [136] He justifies this by citing research from the field of criminal psychology: a fictional scene involving conflict was acted out in front of students — a punch-up between a professor and a student. Subsequently the participating 'witnesses' had to recount what had occurred. Of thirty people, only four or five were able to describe the events in a way that approximated to the reality: 'Most write down far-fetched things if such an event has surprised them.' [137]

But why is this? Why, in such situations, do people not remember what happened, or only in fragments? Their mode of perception has changed: they are disorientated. In relation to this, here's a paragraph from *The Gift of Dyslexia:*

Dr. Stephen Kosslyn, a Harvard University psychologist, says the visual centre of the brain contains a 'visual buffer' where images are perceived and sent to the upper conceptual centres of the brain for processing. The converse also occurs when thoughts and stored visual images are sent back to the visual buffer. There they are perceived as visual images for purposes of recognition by what he also calls 'the mind's eye.'

The real and mental images can be combined and confused, he says. An example is the fact that eyewitnesses of crimes or accidents often believe they saw what their expectations told them to see — not what actually happened. [138]

To cope with daily life or, as Steiner puts it in this context, 'to be able to properly participate in human culture,' one needs to find one's bearings. Repeated retelling therefore does not just practise speech facility but also provides an ideal orientation training. It also gives children with pronounced right-hemisphere tendencies a concept for linear sequences (= L mode). Although they have a whole overview, retelling forces them to bring everything into sequence.

If one wishes to develop the ability to retell through the use of fictional stories, certain fairy tales are especially suited for this since they are defined by their origins in vernacular and oral traditions. They were originally passed on from one person to another by memory, from generation to generation. Fixed in written form they are, strictly speaking, no longer really folk tales as such. By nature they do not require literacy skills but instead a good memory.

In former times people 'knew' about brain-friendly learning, even without detailed insight into it; in other words they knew how one can remember something well. The pronounced pictorial nature of the language of folk tales (= R mode) and the linear development of the events they portray (= L mode) with ever-repeating narrative patterns in a certain sequence (e.g. the eldest son sets off into the world, then the middle son and then the youngest son ...) means that folk tales are inherently brain-friendly.

They can be absorbed, stored and retold in accordance with the brain's natural capacities, as long as one allows them to remain folk- or fairy tales which activate the children's imaginative level (= R mode) and allow them to immerse themselves in the, for children, absolutely 'real' world of unicorns. This does not work if these stories are used instead as tools for a kind of learning which demands that the children surface from the R mode and activate the L mode. To learn letters, the child must enter into reality: one must reach him in his real experience, not in his imagination or fantasy, so that he can then connect this with abstract letters.

Rudolf Steiner, at least, was rigorously consistent in demanding a relation to daily realities when introducing literacy. Hearing folk tales and stories, on the other hand, he regards as 'lifting' children (and others too!) out of and away from reality. He equates it with 'the activity people unfold when asleep' and elsewhere states:

For this reason, folk tales offer wonderful mental and spiritual nourishment at every age. When we tell children suitable folk tales, we stimulate the child's soul in a way that avoids it having always only to adapt to the mode of external reality when confronted by some concept or other.

Such a relationship to reality, in fact, renders the soul arid and empty. The soul preserves the freshness of life, in contrast, so that this soul can fully penetrate our whole organism, when it feels the reality, in a higher sense, at work in the lawfulness of folk tale images. These lift the soul, however, far off and away from the external world. [139]

Folk tales lift us away from the external world not only because of their qualities of form; their content and its sequences also often represent or embody a route from the L to the R mode. Steiner illustrates this in his account of the folk tale of a young boy and a cat, a story which corresponds to the *Puss in Boots* type of tale. He sees in it the following symbolism:

Yes, in the present day you can say that we are really the poor lad in comparison with other times, and have nothing but a clever cat.

But we certainly have the clever cat, for this is our reason, our intellect ... and it's all we have; and it is just about able to get itself up on two feet in order to promise us a certain imaginary possession ...

But we are not just that poor lad. That's what we are in our state of consciousness. But our 'I' is rooted in concealed depths of the soul. These hidden depths of soul are connected with countless worlds and countless cosmic processes, all of which play into our lives.

But nowadays the human being has become a poor boy and knows nothing about all that any more. At most a clever cat, philosophy, can explain to him all sorts of things about the purpose and significance of what he sees with his eyes or his other senses.

And if someone nowadays wishes to speak of something that goes further than the world of the senses, goes beyond it, then he does so — and has already been doing so for many centuries — in art and poetry. [140]

Immersing oneself in fairy tales allows one to enter the depths of 'countless worlds.' Folk and fairy tales demonstrate the strange phenomenon that comparable narrative strands appear all over the world quite independently of one another.

In the fifties and sixties this insight led to efforts to categorize folk tales according to motifs and types. Since then, each has been identified by an 'AT' number. [141]

There are also motifs that surface independently of time and cultural specifics and contain the same symbolism. I encountered one such motif several times while studying the theme of this book — I mention it here only as an observation that astonished me, without wishing to draw any conclusions or contextualize it.

In order to clarify the process of perception activated in disorientation, Ronald Davis recounts the example of the 'ball of fluff' that turns out to be a kitten.[142] As an example of the wholly abstract world of letters he chooses the three-letter word 'cat':

Little P.D.—A Developmental Theory of Dyslexia

Forty dyslexic variations of the word CAT.

Hermann Ehmann also uses the image of a cat to clarify his visualization technique; and Rudolf Steiner sees the clever cat as symbol of reason and intellect, which helps us to understand the world of mind or spirit. Pure coincidence? Perhaps we should all take the trouble to research the 'cat' motif more carefully in relation to its worldwide symbolism. The cat was already sacred to the Egyptians.

To conclude my thoughts on the theme of folk tales, I'd like to continue the quotation from Steiner I gave above, since it seems to me a good summary. You need to remember, though, that when he speaks of 'the present' he's talking about 1911.

But our present time — a period in many respects of such strange transition — truly shows us how mostly we do not feel our way very far beyond the mood of the 'poor lad,' even if he's able to bring poetry and art into the modern, sense-based world as it confronts him.

In our time, out of a certain lack of belief in a higher form of art and poetry, people turn to naturalism, to a purely external reproduction of outer reality.

And who would deny that something in our time responds to these depictions of reality in art and poetry by sighing that all this is just chimera, with no underlying truth?

Doesn't such a mood really inhabit our times? In fact the king in us, who has his origin in the spirit, the world of mind and spirit, needs a lot of persuading by the clever cat, by the reason we possess today, to see that what arises from imagination and awakens in art is in a certain sense a true, human quality and possession.

Initially the king in us is overlaid and drowned out. But that really doesn't achieve much, or only for a little while. Then at a certain point — and it is at the beginning of such a period that we live now — the human being needs to start finding access again to the higher, spiritual world.

This need makes itself felt, and can be felt everywhere today: an urge to rise again into the spheres of mind and spirit, into the world of spirit. A certain period of transition has to occur. And this transition can scarcely be undergone more easily than by re-awakening ai.d re-enlivening the mood of folk tales. [143]

From writing to reading

Steiner bases the acquisition and use of literacy in Class One (age six/seven) on two foundations:

On the one hand, he develops writing from painting and drawing, from pictures of the letters, so that children gain an awareness of the shape of each one. Linked to this he uses observations on sentences and words to clarify the purpose of sentence, word, letter through to phonic sound, allowing the children to experience this through their own manual, imitative activity in painting, modelling and writing. In this way a sense of the fine motor skills required is also heightened, an awareness he began to encourage at the very beginning with exercises involving straight and curved lines.

This procedure reflects the development of writing in human evolution: from the Egyptians' initial picture symbols to the phonic identifiers of our Latin alphabet. Steiner even recapitulates the reversal of letter shapes in his example of the D (*Dach* = roof), which for me parallels laterality development in our culture.

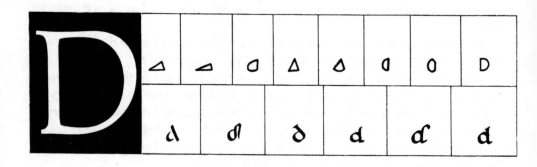

Reading left to right:

Top row:
Early northern Semitic
Phoenician
Early Hebrew
Early Greek
Classical Greek
Early Etruscan
Early Roman
Classic Latin

Bottom row:
Cursive capital (Roman)
Cursive minuscule (Roman)
Anglo-Irish capital
Carolingian minuscule
Venetian minuscule (Italian)
North-Italian minuscule (Roman)

On the other hand, he nurtures use of language — also without the written medium — through the retelling of stories and exercises involving proper expression and pronunciation, for which he also advocates specific speech exercises.[144]

The transition from orality to literacy embodies the development from oral traditions of poetry and narrative (i.e. fairy and folk tales, legends and fables, and the recounting of actual events) through to the simple recording of facts. According to the mercantile theory, the first alphabetic symbols were probably initially developed and used to compile lists.[145] Only later did the use of written script follow as medium for communication and poetry.

Towards the end of Class One, Rudolf Steiner gradually builds up use of writing based on these two foundations, in order to lead children from writing to reading. His aim is:

> ... to ensure that, in a simple way, the child is able to put down on paper this or that spoken by the teacher, or what he himself decides to write down. One should keep it simple, and lead it into the child also being able to read simple things. There is absolutely no need to try to get the child to achieve something complete in this first year. In fact that would be mistaken.
>
> It is much more a matter, in this first year, of bringing the child to the stage of no longer regarding printed text as somehow entirely strange or unknown; and of developing in him a capacity to write down something simple unaided. This, if I can put it like this, would be the ideal for lessons in language and literacy.[146]

Here, too, I recognize parallels with the development of our alphabet: purposeful writing of one's own starts by writing down something or other of a simple nature.

But if one has anything to do with dyslexic children, even such a minimal expectation sounds like the loftiest utopia. One has to stand by and see how, a long time after Class One, letters remain a closed secret for these children, and how, for years, they continue to look upon printed text as something entirely alien.

On the other hand, I am fairly sure that this goal could be achievable if, in the steps described above, one opens up this world of letters to children in a way that corresponds to cultural evolution and is, in addition, 'brain friendly'.

Even though I myself cannot yet cite any of my own experiences in this regard (inevitably I always work with children who are 'already' dyslexic) I'd like to refer here to experiences which might be of use when it comes to engaging, in a simple way initially, with the world of written language; and to do so without losing the pictorial nature of thinking but instead developing it further:

In the 1996 summer issue of *Dyslexia Reader,* there is a report on a Mrs Steel, who was teaching a Class One group, as a pilot class in the Davis symbol mastery method. After learning the alphabet, the class has 'modelling days' on two days each week.

The children then engage with the so-called trigger words, learning that this helps them to understand the meaning of words and to remember things.

To accompany this they formulate and write down simple sentences in their exercise books:

Lori: 'My favourite word is "the" — my word is: the bird is in the cage.'
Chloe: 'I like the word "and." Mrs Steel puts up a word. We make a sentence. I
   made Mum and Dad.'
Kaylee: 'My favourite word is "a." I did a puppy can run.'

The children's formulations may be simple but they are very expressive of their own world, the meaning of concepts and the pictorial nature of language. Most of their texts, in addition, are illustrated with pictures. What is also remarkable is the special sense of motivation triggered by this method — working with all senses and the modelling and artistic aspect.

Sonya: 'Clay makes me feel creative. It keeps my hands cool. Clay keeps your
   hands busy. When I do clay it makes me feel good.'
Megan: 'Clay makes me feel like an artist.'
Leila: 'When I grow up I want to be a clay teacher.'

The children wrote down all these sentences themselves. Not all of it was spelled correctly, but the trigger words were all written properly. At the end of this first school year, the children achieved significantly high levels in a reading text (word recognition text containing about 50 words). The class average in the two symbol mastery groups was 98.5 and 98.9 per cent.

This is all the more striking given that official documentation (by the US National Institute of Child Health and Human Development) showed that one in five children suffers from reading difficulties. One also has to remember that in English, written text diverges from phonetic sound considerably more than in German.

My experiences with dyslexic children have shown me that the route from symbol mastery through to writing one's own text and then on to reading can often be a way to re-motivate frustrated dyslexics, especially younger children. Older, often 'over-therapied' children, who are caught up in the net of their 'old solutions' have a much more difficult time.[147]

Younger children relate well to the artistic mode of expressing themselves in clay; and, after they've modelled in clay, they like writing down 'something simple,' for this too corresponds with their inherent creativity. They no longer face something 'entirely alien.'

In this way many little stories have arisen in my sessions, which their proud authors enthusiastically read out. Here, for instance, about the word 'there':

Peter calls: 'Mummy, there is a dog!'
Marianne says: 'No, Peter, that is a sheep.'
'Because it is eating grass?' Marianne laughs.

Or about the word 'from':

'Hello, Frank!'
'Hello Lola!'
'Oh, where did you find that lovely shell?'
'I got it from Grandma.'
'And where did Grandma get the shell?'
'She found it at the seaside when she was a child.'

Ricarda, age 9

The content of these little, self-invented stories also shows in a wonderful way how important 'complete ideas' are to the children. I gained a particularly deep insight into the special mode of thinking of a thirteen-year-old dyslexic in the first story she wrote after symbol mastery of the word 'in':

I dream well, I dream a lot. Sometimes I dream almost all day. It's called daydreaming. My dreams often give me answers. Just today at school I didn't know whether 'IN the chest' has an 'h' or not.

So I dreamed up a story about the word IN, and at last I knew how IN is written. In the meantime everyone else had finished, but I made up for that by writing IN properly, without asking anyone. But what I dreamed is my secret, and I'm not telling anyone.

I repeatedly find that dyslexic children and teenagers who have often been diagnosed as having pronounced 'learning and developmental disorders' suddenly develop capacities one would never have imagined — especially in the realm of language. Difficulties with written language are all too often *not* attributable to lack of understanding or poor usage of speech and language.

In fact I found that the opposite was true, for instance when a thirteen-year-old — who usually finds it hard to express himself, and often struggles to find words — asked me whether he could write a poem instead of a text relating to the trigger word we had been working on.

This has meanwhile given rise to many poems; here's one example:

Always
Always, always I must work
can't rest when I'm home, can't shirk.
Every morning, dot of 8
in comes teacher, will not wait,
says: 'Get going now and take
care your work is not done late!
I'll teach you what is well worth learning,
whether reading, maths or writing.'
Then we sweat the whole day through
but there is always more to do.
And when I get back home again
doing homework's such a pain.
Doing homework after school
makes me furious, makes me lose my cool!
Always, always I must work,
can't rest when at home, can't shirk.

Stimulated by the children's creative writing, recently I have tried harder to nurture these gifts. I found valuable suggestions in the book by Gabriele L. Rico (see bibliography). Teenage dyslexics, who previously could barely be motivated to write, found they had a talent for writing they would never have thought possible.

I was less surprised myself at these discoveries since the intensive course referred to is based on activating pictorial ideas and images. The methods suggested there are derived from brain-research findings relating to our right-hemisphere creative abilities, and draw strongly on them. But the actual pieces of writing that emerged following the adolescents' discovery of their talent for writing far exceeded all my expectations. I have included additional examples in Appendix I. Here I will just give a piece by a seventeen-year-old, who had been practically illiterate until he was fifteen. In April 1999 he wrote down his thoughts about the war in Kosovo:

War
So many people who weep
and then fall silent and keep
silent about what they've experienced:
which leads to more war.
So many people who keep
suffering, always suffering more.

Gabriele L. Rico's methods of teaching creative writing — especially the 'clustering procedure' she mentions in her book — have recently been used by a Waldorf teacher for teaching poetry classes to fifteen- and sixteen-year-olds. Here is his brief report:

...Writing their own poems is a fine experience for students in the poetry and metre main lesson in Class Ten. It's quite common for students initially to feel surprised and inhibited about spontaneously expressing themselves lyrically. The clustering method helps to overcome these difficulties. The students pursue their associations and spontaneous ideas with interest and enjoyment, and enthusiastically develop their own poems. As they gain assurance in lyrical expression, their writing becomes more complex, but not artificially so.

The clustering method also gives students a way in to reading and analysing poems with more motivation. For instance, in reading Nietzsche's poem 'Ecce Homo' they find it easy to recognize the clusters used as metaphors for the human being ...

Alongside children's own creative writing, in which they produce something 'out of themselves,' there is, of course, also simply recording on paper 'this or that spoken by the teacher' — in other words, dictation.

A dictation in German is somewhat easier than in English, since the former has many more words that are written phonically. But for a dyslexic unable, evidently, to draw on an inner language resource, phonic writing is just as difficult. If he is 'oriented' and familiar with the nature of written language, of letters and their sounds, a dyslexic too can write down what he hears spoken — especially if he has also learned to remember words in their entirety (whole-word method).

The thing to remember here is not to dictate overly long passages in one go, since it is important for a dyslexic to hear words with as small an interval as possible before writing them down. When writing their own words, too, dyslexics often accompany what they write with whispering of the text. Writing would certainly be easier if our written language was all phonetic, but such a 'spelling reform' would doubtless be too radical. Unfortunately, therefore, there is nothing for us to do but imitate Rudolf Steiner in citing the conventions according to which words are written: 'That's how the grown-ups do it.' [148]

But however difficult it is for someone with such a thinking mode to write, for example the sound 'ay' differently each time in 'say,' 'weigh' or 'taste,' the visualization technique and symbol mastery method, equally, helps them to get individual words under their belt as units that exist independently of each other.

Here are a few tips for spelling and dictation for right-hemisphere children:

Visualization exercises for spelling (also suited for learning vocabulary):

- A difficult word is written on the board. The pupils should look at it and picture it.
- The board is shut.
- Various questions are asked about what the word looks like, such as: How many letters have descenders, and how many ascenders? How many vowels does the word have? How many ns? How many curves? etc.
- The word is spelled forwards and backwards (NOTE: not phoneticized!)

Further tips can be found in: Jeffrey Freed / Laurie Parsons: *Right-Brained Children in a Left-Brained World*, Prentice Hall & IBD, 1998

Learning vocabulary with file cards

- The English word is written on one side of the file card and on the other the word in a foreign language. Next to this the pupil sketches a small picture which he himself connects with the meaning of the word.
IMPORTANT: the sketch should represent the child's own idea.

Dictation exercises

Material: short, interesting text, paper, pencil/rubber or fountain pen/tippex

1. Self-dictation (for pupils with major spelling difficulties, but also suitable
   for foreign-language learning)

A) The text is read or read out.
B) Anything unclear is explained.
C) Look at the first word. IMPORTANT: The pupil must be able to read and
   understand the word.
D) Look upwards (to the top right or left — some also look diagonally
   downwards; it is best for each pupil to find what suits him by trying it out).
E) Picture the letters of the word *there*.
F) If unsure, compare again with the word.
G) Write down the *pictured* word.
H) Compare the word you have written with the original.
I) Do the same with each subsequent word.

To begin with the text should be short (1–2 sentences) and then increase
slowly to 4 sentences. Over time, several words can be 'pictured between.' Doing
this is important as the sequence of letters can thus become anchored in long-
term memory.

2. Smiley ☺ dictation (foreign-language dictation)

Understanding phase:
•   A short text is read out. Any issues of understanding are clarified.

Dictation phase:
•   The text is dictated, word by word if possible.
•   The pupil pictures each word and then writes it down. A line of
    space is always left between each line of writing.

Reflection phase:
•   After the dictation, the pupil underlines words in colour (e.g. green) where
    he is *unsure* if they are written properly.

Correction and learning phase:
•   The text is handed out.
•   The pupil compares his dictation with the original and underlines words
    written wrongly in yellow.

- If words underlined in green ('unsure') are right, the pupil draws a ☺ over the word.
- For words that need correcting, two columns are created below the text:
- WHK (= would have known) and WNHK (= would not have known)
- The pupil now decides — depending on whether he would or would not have known how to spell a word — which column to assign words to, writing them with their proper spelling.
- With help of 'between picturing,' all words are now spelled both forwards and backwards, and where necessary written down again.

The reflection phase ('where am I unsure?') enables the pupil to engage again with what has been written, and motivates him to check it himself. This correction phase is the most important part of the dictation, since it is where something really new is learned.

It is somewhat surprising that Rudolf Steiner suggests giving dictation to children at such an early stage, for this exercise is much more commonly used to check children's spelling rather than to help them learn the process of writing.

As far as I am aware, dictation is used extensively in Waldorf schools, but usually only once processes of writing and learning to read are regarded as largely completed. And even if such dictation — unlike in mainstream schools — does not necessarily serve to check children's spelling, it has a markedly different function to that initiated by Rudolf Steiner.

It simply replaces another form of engagement with written language involving 'writing from the board' which in many Waldorf schools occupies a good deal of time in the first years of school — long before children are expected to be able to cope with dictation.

It seems that many dyslexic children can also copy beautifully from the board, with regard to spelling and handwriting. However this tends to cover up their problems with written language for a long time.

But what kind of activity does this actually involve? One could just as well have got them to copy Nordic runes or Arabic symbols, and they would have done it just as beautifully and 'correctly.' What does not happen is any inner participation in understanding what they copy down.

Many, indeed, fulfil this task with astonishing skill, but they are not involved in a process that leads from copying to reading, and then from reading to proper writing, for in order to understand what they copy they would require reading skills. And the older they grow, the more bored they get with this senseless copying. In addition, they become ever less able to keep up with the increasing speed with which the others can copy, and so their own rather lovely handwriting-drawing becomes an ever less legible scribble.

Anyone who has, like me, spent some time working with dyslexic Waldorf pupils, will soon recognize the problem. So I asked myself why (since that is what I had to assume) Rudolf Steiner considered 'copying from the board' a methodological approach of enough significance to assign it a good portion of the school day. In my search I did finally discover a reference to copying from the board. But before I examine this further, I'd like to take a look for a moment at the very different activities of writing and copying.

The DUDEN dictionary (DER GROSSE DUDEN, volume 10) defines them as follows:

Write, wrote, written	Copy, copied, has copied
1. *Place letters, numbers, figures in a certain sequence on paper or similar:* Learn to write, write well or properly; write with ink; write a note	1. *a) write again (something that is already present in written form):* copy a passage from a book; *b) copy illicitly:* He copied it from his neighbour

And here is Rudolf Steiner's recommendation relating to what he refers to as 'taking down' or 'transcribing' (German = *nachschreiben*) rather than 'copying':

Now after we have derived and accentuated certain things [he is referring to the letters, such as the F from the picture of the fish] from the whole human being, then we must begin to get the child to see that grown-ups, when they see these strange shapes in front of them, discover a meaning in them by developing further the single details the child has now learned; and then we pass on — no matter whether the child understands each single aspect or not — to writing down sentences.

In these sentences the child will now see certain shapes such as he became acquainted with in the fish. At the same time he will also notice other shapes, which due to time constraints we can't now derive in the same way from other objects.

Then we will start drawing on the board to show how individual letters appear when they're printed; and one day we will write down a long sentence on the board, and say to the child: this is what the grown-ups see in front of them when they have learned and developed all that we talked about when we found the f in the fish etc.

Then we will teach the child how to transcribe. We will make sure that what he sees passes into his hands — so that he doesn't just read it with his eyes, but forms it subsequently with his hands; and so that he knows that he himself can also form everything on the board in the same way. In other words, he will not learn to read without forming with his hand what he sees before him, i.e. the written shape of letters. In this way we achieve something of very great importance, namely that the child never reads just with the eye, but that his eye activity passes into the whole of his limb activity.

Then children will feel unconsciously, right into their legs, what they otherwise only take in with their eyes. What we must seek in this activity is to engage the whole human being. And then we take the reverse route: we take apart the sentence we have written, and we show the shapes of the other letters which we have not yet derived from their elements, by atomizing words: in other words we pass now from the whole to the individual components. For example: here we have 'head.' First the child learns to write 'head' simply transcribing it as if drawing. And now we split the word 'head' up into h, e, a, d, deriving the single letters from the whole word; we pass from the whole to the single parts ... [149]

These comments on 'transcribing' can certainly be used as grounds for the methodology of copying, but we have to note that Rudolf Steiner expressly relates it to the introduction of print characters which, as was common in his time, he only envisaged after introduction of Roman cursive characters. In other words, the activity of transcribing is geared to learning the alphabet, to practising the shapes of the letters, not to actual proper writing or reading. He is concerned here with letters and their appearance in words and sentences.

In my view, therefore, Steiner's 'transcribing' also corresponds more to the Duden definition of 'writing' rather than 'copying,' whereas the common method of copying at Waldorf schools (as far as I am familiar with it) falls under the definition for 'copying.' At least, I do not see Steiner's comments about copying from the board as a suggestion that this should be perpetuated for years, and that long texts should be copied.

Transcribing, as Steiner recommends it, can certainly be seen as an R-mode activity: a calligraphic, artistic way of taking down words. But with words and whole sentences a domain of the L mode is added, which is of enormous importance in relation to the desired skill of reading: a linear movement carried out from left to right. In other words, transcribing is important for the acquisition of script symbols, but not for the use of written language: it is a basic training that can also be carried out and supported by modelling the letters.

Once the child is familiar with the activity of writing, and perhaps even simple reading (but more of a copying and drawing activity than anything) this should not then degenerate into a mechanical kind of text-copying.

In this connection I found a characteristic remark by Rudolf Steiner — not expressly stated in his lectures on education, but in his *Autobiography*:

While the lads in my row had to copy down the story of King Arpad, the really little ones stood at a board where I and U had been written for them in chalk. It was simply impossible to do anything other than let the soul stew in lethargy or despondency, and undertake this copying almost mechanically. [150]

There is no inner participation in mechanical copying of texts — unless one has a certain interest in the content. If it has any use in learning, then only for pupils who have the capacity to inwardly speak the text as they transcribe it — in other words, they have to be able to read already. Then they may perhaps improve their reading skills and spelling.

Since most of us — especially most teachers — are predominantly verbal thinkers, Steiner's formula of 'from writing to reading' has also probably been automatically misunderstood as 'from copying to reading' and similarly put into practice, especially since this gives rise to beautifully designed, though not especially 'individual' or individually creative main lesson books. For most children the method has clearly worked; however I believe that these children would have learned to read and write by more or less any method.

But to be able to take personal possession of written language and use it, to master it, inner participation must be an ingredient. Only then can one's own world of ideas, images and thoughts — whether verbally conceived or non-verbally perceived — come to expression and communicate themselves to others.

The activity of writing (1st foundation) is connected with use of language (2nd foundation). This connection can then be more strongly developed over time by making a careful transition to recounting stories and descriptions:

And when the second school year approaches, one will try to continue and further develop the telling of stories and getting the children to re-tell them.
In Class Two the child can gradually be led to writing down what one relates.

Does Steiner here mean the writing down of a retold story, or of a dictation? I suspect that he envisages both possibilities, but certainly not mechanical copying from the board.

He is much more concerned, instead, to establish a connection between acquiring the basic components of written language and their usage, which initially consists in written retelling. The child must be creative in the choice of words, but has already practised this in verbal retelling; and above all he has a complete idea and picture of the content.

And then, after the child has learned to write down what one recounts, one can get him to make very short descriptions of what he has learned about animals, plants, and the local environment such as meadow and wood. [151]

The following remark shows how important it was for Rudolf Steiner that the child should be individually active and attentive when writing, so that the soul would not 'stew in lethargy':

... If we teach the child eurythmy, if we get him to sing, get him to make music, to do gymnastics — and even if we get him to write, insofar as he develops self-directed activity — or when we get him to handwork, an activity is involved which we can compare with wakefulness: an enhanced wakefulness arises. [152]

This self-directed activity with inner participation almost automatically leads in writing to also wanting and being able to read. I myself have often experienced this: dyslexic children happily and proudly read out to me the sentences they themselves have formulated, and their own little stories.

I am fairly certain that Rudolf Steiner was referring to this very route from writing to reading:

Now the child has arrived at a certain point of development. He speaks and can fix in writing what he says. Only then has the time arrived to start practising reading, to teach reading. And this reading will be easy to learn if one has first developed writing to what, in a certain sense, can be called a full level.

Then if the child has practised the content of what is written and read by locating it within himself, in the motor system, the movement system, and was inwardly engaged in developing what is then to be the reading matter, then he is also ready to cope with doing something one-sided. Without any danger for human development, the head can now be called upon to transpose into reading what the child has first learned to fix in writing. [153]

This passage sounds as if Steiner had already taken the measure of modern brain research. Only when, by integrating the modes of both hemispheres, thorough understanding of the structure of our script has been developed and active engagement with writing has been practised; when the child has participated inwardly in the development of what is to be read, without stewing in lethargy or mechanical hand facility; when he has practised incorporating the content of what is written into the motor system, is he then ready to do something more one-sided: is ready for the activity of reading which, after all, is a one-sided activity of the left hemisphere, for reading is initially a linear observation of single sounds that must be decoded as words.

The sense and holistic grasp of reading matter is — especially in German — often only possible when you reach the end of the sentence. Even if they learn more slowly, children introduced to reading in this way will not only have fewer literacy problems to battle with, but will also no doubt be able to engage in a more differentiated way with texts and text content.

Remembering and integrating non-verbal thought structures with the aid of Davis's symbol mastery has already given rise to astonishing results. Children who thereby develop the habit of forming clear pictorial ideas or also feeling concepts of words, will no longer so readily swallow empty or meaningless phrases. First findings from the pilot classes have also demonstrated that they are better at searching texts for meaning:

'They learn that there is more to reading than just decoding words ... A boy found the word "would" in his reading book and said: "I have found the word 'would' but it doesn't have the right meaning."

In Class Two [age six/seven] reading becomes more than just learning a series of words by heart. They notice that these little words help them to understand the story.

Watching children at this age pondering critically on the use of language, or discussing tenses of verbs and giving commentaries on punctuation, is phenomenal and at the same time heart-warming.'[154]

I would like to add a few things here about the handwriting of right-hemisphere children.

Repeatedly, I found to my surprise that these children try to learn joined-up writing from an early age. Even when their fine motor skills seem to make it hard for them to write block letters they master cursive letters astonishingly well. Joined-up writing, with its dynamic forms, corresponds to their right-hemisphere mode of thinking. I now believe that it would be better for writing lessons to start with the learning of cursive script.

This new approach did not come easily to me. In the first edition of this book I engaged with this problem but could not find any real explanation of why Rudolf Steiner recommends cursive script over block script. The only, rather feeble, explanation I found was connected with the additional problem represented by German gothic script used at the time.

Today, though, I am entirely in agreement with Steiner's method:

It would be a natural thing for us to gradually seek a transition from drawn shapes to the cursive script. If we are in a position to start with the cursive script, we should definitely do so, for only then will we be able to lead the cursive (Roman) script into German script. And after the child has learned to write and read simple written forms, enlivened through whole words, we can pass to block or print letters. Of course we first take the Roman and then the German script. [155]

Engaging with Reading Texts

Once one can write and read, another aspect of literacy usually comes into play: understanding what one has read — refined by analysis and individualized by interpretation. Yet Rudolf Steiner once again proceeds the other way round:

> *I'd like to point out that you should never spoil the feeling and sense of a reading text — if I can call it by that prosaic name — by reading the piece out or reading it with the children, and then pedantically explaining it ...*
>
> *That's why it's always good to embark on actually reading a piece as the last thing of all, preceding this with everything you want to do in the way of making it comprehensible.[156]*

This is actually a very unusual way of working with texts, especially if you intend continuing like this at all ages, right into secondary school. Most of us would consider the other way round more logical: first reading then analysing and interpreting. That's also how we've been taught.

But Steiner gives an example of how you can work with texts in a different way. It is fascinating how, before the children embark on a reading text, he characterizes figures who they will encounter in it. Here, too, he always proceeds from an idea of the whole and involves the child addressed, with his personal scope of experience, in his commentary: 'Dear children, I'm sure you've seen dogs before in your life ...'

In complete pictures he describes in advance the various characters — in this case the appearance and designated tasks of the types of dog who figure in the tale. Then he makes connections with related types of human behaviour. So really, before they start to read, the children are familiar with everything: they can already 'see' the dogs and their circumstances, and connect with them in their minds (they themselves are 'in the picture'); all that remains to be discovered is how the characters will interact. Reading will then give them the sequence of events.

Such a procedure gives certainty, though it certainly does not correspond to the linear structure of our 'scientific norm.' From a totality (= R mode) it directs the focus to details (= L mode) — a reciprocal effect which allows integrative and analogous processing. The ideas/images previously developed can then be connected with a text. Language connected with images and feelings — a truly brain-friendly method!

Steiner himself justifies his conviction like this:

If one gave the children the following little tale without any explanation, they would not be wholly prepared since their feelings and emotions would not yet have been directed towards what it involves. If one were only to give explanations afterwards, this would pedantically dissipate it, and they would not be able to read it properly either. [157]

In other words, his recommendations are not just about proper understanding of what the children read but also about proper reading itself. Expressed in Davis's terminology this would be stated as: after an initial explanation no concepts met in the text will be unknown, such as could confuse and disorientate the predominantly non-verbal thinkers at least. And with growing orientation, reading facility grows.

This method of approaching reading texts, as Steiner here elaborates, appears at first glance to contradict other statements by him, since he frequently emphasizes how important it is to speak with children in a way that they don't immediately understand.[158] Instead they should initially feel an 'inkling of the mysteries of existence.' He warns against 'filling them too full with rational concepts.'

But if we examine more carefully his explanations relating to the afore-mentioned story (with the different types of dog), he does not give any rational concept definitions but pictorial descriptions that render concepts visible and accessible to feeling. There is also a significant difference between telling children something they do not yet understand in every detail, and them reading merely incomprehensible words.

In the first case a dyslexic can, for instance with the aid of his disorientation function, form his own images and feelings in relation to what he hears. Even if these are perhaps not clearly defined, he often acquires an inkling of the content and thus expands his intuitive memory.

As a mother of dyslexic children, I often hear comments such as 'I know what you mean, but I can't explain it properly' when I ask if they've understood something in a story I'm reading to them. However, when they read a text on their own, and it contains unfamiliar terms, use of the disorientation function leads in contrast straight into the void. [159]

Speech not wholly understood is not problematic for a child, and is even desirable, for that's how he learned his mother tongue. In addition, spoken language is usually accompanied by mime, intonation etc. (= R mode), and verbal or non-verbal queries can be used to get a better idea of what is not yet understood.

In written language, on the other hand, one is dependent on the phonic identifiers (= L mode), and to decipher them one needs to know their meaning.

For work with Davis's symbol mastery, the first essential step is therefore to define the concept of a word. With the aid of a dictionary or encyclopaedia, the dyslexic tries to gain an idea of the term through definitions and illustrative sentences, which he then turns into clay models. Thus each person can individually and age-appropriately create his meaning pictures and associate them with the corresponding written word. The capacity of analogy will later enable these to be enhanced to additional, more complex levels. A purely logical definition would not give the dyslexic any real access.

The definition only serves as a basis for a general understanding of the concept (convention), while its use in illustrative sentences gives clarity about its meaning. Transforming it into a clay model that one makes oneself, is what leads to real control and mastery of a term that previously had no pictorial association.[160]

'If we model the concept of a word in clay, what we are really doing is creating this concept in the real world.'[161]

Rudolf Steiner also regards isolated definitions as too one-sided:

'Yes, of course, definitions are very useful, but also almost always very one-sided. What's important is to find our way directly into life.'

Barbara Meister Vitale draws on a range of techniques to facilitate holistic understanding of texts. For instance, she recommends first discussing any illustrations and also letting the children gain visual familiarity with the text — for instance by asking them first about single words or certain punctuation marks, or getting them to look for certain words such as names. Vera Birkenbihl makes similar suggestions for 'brain-friendly learning'. [162]

Ronald Davis, in addition, suggests a 'third step in learning to read':

Stop briefly at a punctuation mark and visualize or develop a feeling about what has been read. Every complete thought can either be felt or represented as a picture.[163]

Here he concurs with Vera Birkenbihl, who also recommends the language visualization method, since:

The only purpose of reading is to understand what is read. Reading without full and complete comprehension of what is read is the source of most misunderstanding in any subject at any level. [164]

Techniques for increasing reading speed also deserve special attention. These are derived from brain-research findings and are often used in management training courses, e.g. the 'Speed Reading' Programme devised by Tony Buzan.

My first experiences with this taught me that this mode of reading corresponds to the way dyslexics perceive things. Max (age sixteen), with whom I started the programme, described his experiences as follows after completing about one third of the course:

Speed Reading is a means to enhance reading speed and increase understanding of a text.

With Speed Reading I tripled my reading speed and improved my understanding by ten percent. In Speed Reading you're meant to look at several words simultaneously, then pass your gaze over the page in zigzag fashion (from above downwards).

You don't get everything at once, but you're surprised when you find how much you did pick up.

Buzan himself mentions similar experiences with dyslexics and so-called 'attention-deficit disorders.' But this is probably not a method that can simply be applied to everyone regardless, and further research is needed.

However, these first experiences may explain Rudolf Steiner's 'ease at reading' to which he refers on several occasions, and which he probably taught himself. For many this facility seemed mysterious:

Besides all this creative work which he continued from his sickbed day after day, Rudolf Steiner read an extraordinary amount during these months ... it's a mystery when he found time to study the huge pile of books ... alongside all his work, and despite his illness; but from occasional remarks he made at the next book review session, it was clear that he knew their contents thoroughly. [165]

Thinking About Grammar

Rudolf Steiner wove many noteworthy comments on grammar teaching into his lectures. The book (in German) compiled by Erich Gabert, entitled *List of Comments by Rudolf Steiner on Grammar Teaching*, contains a very good overview of these. It also includes suggestions for grammar in foreign-language teaching.

However, Gabert himself says that his compilation is not complete since he did not include Steiner's detailed lectures on language and philology. [166] What is also important is to always read the comments in their original context.

Steiner stresses repeatedly that grammar should not be taught in an abstract way but should be developed in a living way from language itself. He refers to the 'feeling' and 'sculptural' elements in language — which strikes one as somewhat odd in relation to grammar.

Like most people, I can recall fairly dry, theoretical grammar lessons, without much feeling content, in which written language was considered and analysed in an abstract way. Only when I discovered Steiner's explanations relating to different types of words did I start to grasp the 'plastic' nature of grammar, at the same time encountering a procedure I had meanwhile become acquainted with, but which, equally, remained problematic:

We must also teach the child what a noun is and an article. And now we find ourselves in a real calamity, for according to the curriculum here, we should use the German expressions and not say 'article.'*

According to government regulations we must use the term 'gender word'** and this of course is a dire situation. It would be better if people weren't so pedantic and allowed us to retain the word 'article.'

Now I have suggested to you how to distinguish for the child between a 'noun' and an 'adjective' by getting him to see that the noun in a certain sense relates to what exists externally in spatial terms, stands there as it were.

---

*   *Artikel* in German, which is derived from Latin.

**   *Geschlechtswort* — since both definite and indefinite articles in German are one of three 'genders' (masculine, feminine and neuter).

*One must try to say to the child something like this: 'Look, there's a tree. A tree is something that stands there outside. But if you look at a tree in winter, or spring, or again in summer you will always see it there, yet it looks different in winter from how it does in summer, and different again in spring. In winter we say: it is brown. In spring we say: it is growing green. In summer we say: it is colourful. Those are its different qualities.'**

In this way we first teach the child the difference between what stays still and constant, and the different qualities, and then we say to him: if we need a word for what stays constant, that's 'noun;' when we need a word for the changing qualities of something, that is an 'adjective.'

*Then we teach the child the concept of activity: 'Sit down on your chair. You are a good child. "Good" is an adjective. But now stand up and run about — you're doing something. That's an activity. We use the word "verb" for this activity.** In other words we try to lead the child to some reality and then we pass on from the reality to the words for it. In this way, without too much damage or difficulty, we will be able to teach the child what a noun, an adjective and a verb are.*

To understand what an article is, is the most difficult thing of all, since the child cannot yet properly grasp the relationship of the article to the noun. We will be forced to splash about in an abstract realm if we wish to teach children what an article is. But they are compelled to learn this. And it is much better to splash about in the abstract — since the whole undertaking is anyway unnatural — than to dream up all kinds of artificial methods to show the child the meaning and nature of the article, which is really impossible. [167]

This commentary once again shows Rudolf Steiner's pictorial, 'dyslexic' mode of thinking. He remains methodologically true to his principles, with wonderful consistency: from introduction of the letters ('You've seen a fish, haven't you?'), through approaching reading ('Dear children, I'm sure you've seen dogs before in your life ...'), to an explanation of the different types of word ('Look, there's a tree').

Here, too, he starts with a picture in which he includes the child, and only then introduces the related concepts. As far as possible he once again develops these from an overall totality by discussing several types of word at the same time and relating them to each other.

A few months ago, when I was going to teach some grammar to a dyslexic, I read out the Steiner extract above — just the beginning of each part, and then formulated the rest in my own words — until he shook his head and pointed to the book: 'Go on reading. I can understand that.'

---

* The word for 'adjective' in German is *Eigenschaftswort* or, literally 'quality word.'
** The German for 'verb' is *Tätigkeitswort* which means 'activity word.'

At the same time, though, this quote also reveals the limitations Rudolf Steiner came up against in using this method to convey the different types of word. Why was he able to convey nouns, adjectives and verbs in such a tangible way, but drew a blank with articles?

Just a few years ago this 'admission' would have been completely incomprehensible to me, for the 'article' comprises only five little words in German: the definite article '*der, die, das*' ('the' in English) and the indefinite article '*ein, eine*' ('a' in English). Surely these wouldn't be too hard to remember!

I wonder whether Erika Dühnfort — who in her book (in German), *The Artistry of Language Structure: Grammar in Waldorf Education*, engages otherwise in such a wonderfully detailed way with Steiner's suggestions about grammar — asked herself this question. In fact, it is precisely this passage of the extract that she left out of her observations, only citing the paragraphs I have reproduced in italic script.

She clearly did not foresee one problem connected with teaching the article, for a few sentences later she writes:

> *The articles (required to be taught as 'gender words' in Württemberg primary classes since 1919) present no difficulties if they are considered according to their inherent nature.* [168]

If one experiences how confusing and literally 'inconceivable' these articles are for non-verbal thinkers, and that dyslexics repeatedly stumble over them, it will be clear why the article was also problematic for Steiner.*

What for Steiner was 'the most difficult thing of all' remains so for many today: the articles, along with many prepositions, conjunctions, adverbial definitions, auxiliary and modal verbs and pronouns are among the chief triggers of disorientation in dyslexics. They can only be grasped and 'mastered' if one creates tangible models for them. It is laborious but possible.

© *The Berkeley Publishing Group, New York*

---

* The difficulty is clearly greater in German with its three genders of words.

I am certain that use of symbol mastery in grammar teaching facilitates a more lively and hands-on engagement with language for all children — from basic types of words onwards.

I'd like to give two further examples to show how nouns and adjectives can be depicted in the symbol mastery method:

'Hat'   'Cheerful' or 'happy' © DDA Deutschland

This can be enhanced by other comments from Steiner about types of words. The models above allow us to 'feel' and 'see' what he means. For example, though he states that one 'separates oneself' from an object via the noun, nevertheless, '... by invoking the quality (adjective) I approach it more closely again ...' and '... with the verb I connect my I with the physical body of the other.'[169]

These remarks can be related to others that we discussed earlier about a 'straight line' and a 'curved line' — the quality (adjective) brings the abstract line closer to the child and the activity (verb) creates connection with it. (see p. 97)

(see p. 97)

Dyslexics often also have great difficulties with concepts and words for tenses — for how can one conceive 'the present?' It is either already past or still lies in the future. Here I discovered a lovely, pictorial explanation by Leonardo da Vinci, which leads to an 'Aha' experience for dyslexics: 'If you put your hand in a river, you have just touched the last thing that is past and the first thing about to come. The present moment is the same.'

Digression: Visible Language

So far I have tried to show in detail how Rudolf Steiner bases acquisition and use of literacy skills on two foundations that correspond to processes in human evolution. Alongside this he continually regrets the loss of a 'visible' language (e.g. hieroglyphs) and urges a renewal of language 'visibility' in our times. He wishes to give back to language more of its feeling character, its soul-spiritual element (which is verbally expressed in sounds), through visibly represented tones and sounds:

> *Whereas in written script, which is also a silent language, the element of language separates itself from us, it connects again more intimately if one turns to eurythmy. This lives wholly within us, where we do not fix in a dry symbol what comes to expression in speech, but where instead we ourselves make what lives in language, for instance in poetry, into an artistic tool ...*[171]

My question here is whether eurythmy might exercise a supporting function in acquiring literacy skills. While learning the alphabet, one could also use the speech — sound (letter) gestures of eurythmy to give additional visibility to sound distinctions. This would certainly support non-verbal thinkers in their recognition of speech sounds, and at the same time give all children a greater sense of the feeling qualities in language.

But is an interdisciplinary measure like this worth pursuing? Would it even be practical? Does it make any sense, or would this be misuse of an inherently artistic element? I would be very pleased to hear from anyone who has had experience with this.

I found only a few remarks by Steiner in relation to this idea. He usually only refers to eurythmy as the opposite of gymnastics. However he makes a few comments that link eurythmy gestures with acquiring literacy skills. I found them in his remarks about teaching the vowels to children:

Then there'll be a child, or children, who you'll be able to get to say 'i, i, i." [In *the eurythmy gesture] ... lies the drawn shape of the sound 'I,' clearly expressed.*[172]

And another pointer:

And so, if you place inner soul qualities, particularly eurythmy concepts, before the child, you will enable him to do this, you'll be able to develop the vowels too. Eurythmy will be an enormous help to you here, since the sounds are already formed in eurythmy gestures. Just think of the O — one encompasses and embraces something; one encompasses something lovingly.[173]

Children find it hard to differentiate nuances of vowel sounds because every vowel letter contains a range of possible sounds, especially if one also takes foreign languages into account. Thus, in his discussions with teachers, Rudolf Steiner also mentions using eurythmy in foreign-language teaching:

Language teaching is successful and will be so to a still greater extent the more you manage, here too, to get the children to be active. Here one could also point to eurythmy in foreign languages. Every speech sound lies between two others. The English I (ai) lies between Ah and EE ... Take your lead from the actual sound, not the written letter.[174]

I can only just touch on these thoughts in connection with learning literacy and foreign languages, but interesting links can be found everywhere, and should really be pursued further.

My real reason for this digression was another idea. What is Rudolf Steiner doing when he gets children to make speech sounds in eurythmy? He's making language visible. What is Ronald Davis doing when he gets them to model words? He's likewise making language visible. Language made visible! From visible reality a word is derived in speech, and a symbol in written language; and from the word/symbol as either a model or gesture, visible reality arises again.

Then, in my wanderings through the diversity of forms of expression in language, I encountered a 'visible language' that has not really been rendered visible but which, rather, becomes direct and immediate reality in gesture without passing through speech. From the very outset, then, it is a language without words which, apart from expressing an enhanced sensory quality, elicits a quite particular, pronounced pictorial quality — a pure, non-verbal

---

* English vowel sound = ee

language with a comprehensive set of rules and complex syntactical structure: sign language for the deaf.

The following is stated in a teaching manual for German sign language (GSL):

In the past three decades ... modern linguistics has shown that international sign languages for the deaf are in no way less complex or capable of expressiveness than spoken languages. This likewise applies to GSL. It is not a gestured form of German, or a set of gestures to accompany speech, but possesses its own grammar and specific vocabulary. Both have to be learned for GSL in exactly the same way as the grammar and vocabulary of German speech.

The grammatical structures and rules of GSL, however, follow quite different principles from spoken German. Whereas the spoken language functions via the ear and speech organs, GSL is a visual language that uses the body as speech instrument.

The hand signs or gestures play an especially important role here. In addition, usually simultaneously, mimicry, head and body stance, and the gesturing space in front of the upper torso, are intentionally used to create grammatical signals and functions.

Using GSL one can convey differentiated, complex and abstract thoughts. Signers can discuss philosophy, literature or politics just as well as football, cars or their tax return. The language of gestures can express poetry just as movingly as spoken language.

Even jokes, humour and satire can be conveyed in signing as subtly or bitingly as in speech. In response to cultural and technological advances, new gesturing signs are also continually introduced into GSL from the hearing community.

In other words, signing is a differentiated, spatial and visual form of communication that can be learned like the spoken language if people communicate with the deaf child in this way from an early age. Hearing people can also learn it, like any other foreign language.

Learning sign language might even be of particular interest for people with ordinary hearing: initial practical trials show that non-verbal thinkers or dyslexics might primarily and ideally use their talents in learning this language. The frustration they experience in learning a foreign language would probably not arise here. On the contrary, they are likely to excel.

In future, the profession of signing interpreter might even turn out to be an ideal profession for dyslexics, drawing on their diverse capacities and gifts. But this is only a secondary thought.

What occurred to me spontaneously as a question — or series of questions — as I became acquainted with this entirely foreign language was this: how do deaf people communicate in writing if their 'mother tongue' has no spoken words or sounds? How do they learn the written language of German, which consists, after all, of phonic symbols? How do they learn to read and write without an inner sense of words and sounds? Naturally they have eyes and hands, the tools they need to read and write, but how do deaf people think? Is it related to the way non-verbal thinkers think?

In posing this latter question I finally made the connection, and suspected that education for the deaf might lead me to additional, perhaps hitherto unused methodologies for approaching literacy for non-verbal thinkers in general, which I could apply specifically to my work with dyslexics.

What I discovered was a similar, helpless battle with letters, a stumbling around in the fog of the incomprehensible, very like the one I had experienced in the arduous and (for both learners and teachers) frustrating attempts to help non-verbal thinkers access the world of written language.

In fact, the problem is if anything even more urgent in the realm of deaf education. At the library of the centre for German sign language in Hamburg, I discovered a 1986 project proposal by Dr. S. Prillwitz for a computer-aided language-learning program for children with hearing impairment, where he writes the following:

The importance of making strenuous efforts to help the deaf acquire literacy skills, and of developing new approaches, is demonstrated by all the latest empirical data on reading and writing capacities amongst the deaf. Although the deaf have no intrinsic problem in perceiving written language since it is a visually realized form of language (as distinct from spoken language), the great majority of deaf people achieve only very low levels of ability in reading and writing.

Conrad (1977) in the English-speaking world showed that hearing-impaired children aged around sixteen achieve on average only a reading age of eight. According to his research, almost half of all deaf teenagers leave deaf school illiterate.

Whether the computer program helped get a handle on the problem appears dubious. But as can be seen in more recent research, the work of past years has proven one thing at least: teaching spoken language to the deaf must precede any, however ingenious, methods of teaching written language, since, as communication tool and key to written language, lack of familiarity with the mother tongue will make literacy well-nigh impossible.

It has been proven that deaf children who acquire sign language as their mother tongue pass through the same stages in learning its language as hearing children, and that this has a positive effect on their whole cognitive and emotional development. Hearing children usually only learn reading and writing once they have learned to speak their mother tongue. For this reason, it is hoped that teaching sign language to the deaf will lead to marked improvements in their capacity for literacy.

Today, therefore, efforts have been increased to gain widespread social 'acknowledgment' of sign language, to teach it and use it consistently in ordinary schools. Although it has existed for so long and is such a perfect communication tool, its use is unfortunately by no means a matter of course. In 1880, its use in Europe was actually forbidden, as 'monkey speech' and these attitudes persist.

But though I was premature in thinking I might have found a connection and solution, gestures and/or models can indeed make written language comprehensible to a non-verbal thinker, enabling him to master it by rendering it visible and pictorial.

And if, at present, I have not yet derived any specific educational methodologies *from* deaf teaching for my work with dyslexics, a meeting of sign language and the Davis method, on the one hand, and of the former with Steiner education on the other, might well stimulate developments *for* deaf education.

Why should it not be possible to offer deaf pupils support for literacy through 'making language visible' with symbol mastery of words? What kinds of experience result when deaf people do eurythmy? And, vice versa, what qualities are hidden from hearing people in the visible language of the deaf? What capacities or abilities would we nurture in hearing people if we were to offer sign language as a school subject? Here, at any rate, a whole range of interesting connections opens up. And even if it sounds like utopia at present, maybe sign language could enrich many in the future.

The French director Nicolas Philibert, who actually regards sign language as having the potential to be a world language, says the following about his experiences while making the film *The Land of the Deaf*:

> *Sign language is enormously rich and alive. However, I'm unable to share deaf people's sensory experience ... We have an auditory memory, while they chiefly have a visual one ... Sign language is being developed further on a daily basis. They are continually inventing new signs. Their language has a more sensory quality because facial expressions are also included in it.*[175]

Pictorial Thinking Exercises

Vera Birkenbihl recommends an interesting exercise for co-ordination of the two brain hemispheres involving a short 'sign training' done each day. This is done by drawing or painting mirrored motifs (e.g. a butterfly, a beetle, an umbrella or a suitcase) with both hands at the same time. [176]

Betty Edwards, a drawing teacher, also urges us to draw, suggesting the well-known 'vase faces' technique (*see* picture). For right-handed people she suggests first drawing a face (in profile) on the left-hand side of the sheet of paper; then extending horizontal lines above and below so as to draw the reversed profile on the right-hand side of the sheet. In doing this one should take care only to mirror the shapes and not to inwardly designate the 'facial features' (forehead, nose, chin etc.) as such (= L mode).

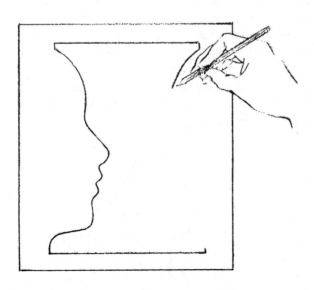

Over time, increasingly complex profiles should then be 'doggedly' contoured: 'The complexity of the form forces the shift to right-hemisphere mode.' [177]

In both these training ideas I find an astonishing parallel once again with a recommendation by Rudolf Steiner: mirror-image form drawing. However, here he wants students to draw 'pure forms' from the outset; in other words abstract shapes without resemblance to named objects in real life, which might invoke use of the L mode (language). He is concerned with engendering a sense of form as such, with a feeling for symmetry and harmony, so as to develop tangible, pictorial thinking (= R mode). He says, 'Let us now consider another branch of pictorial teaching and educating ...' and then shows how one should get a child to finish an unfinished shape as mirror image. He continues, 'The child will first find this very awkward but will gradually, in the balancing activity, develop a thinking sight and seeing thinking. His thinking will remain wholly pictorial.' [178]

Although the mirroring of forms, especially when these represent letters, is part of the natural way in which dyslexics think, they often find it hard to consciously outline forms in 'form drawing.' I suspect that this difficulty is due to the fact that this requires them to leave the disorientation mode — the capacity to picture things and shapes in three dimensions — and to pass instead to a two-dimensional mode.

To reduce the multiple pictures to a single one, however, can be more easily achieved if one has previously been able to make a clear inner picture of the finished form. [179]

If a dyslexic is 'orientated' in this way, he can perceive symmetry and harmony precisely. By approaching things in this manner, form drawing can promote and nurture pictorial thinking (= R mode) and also, simultaneously, serves as an orientation aid for children with dyslexic tendencies, and for integrating the two hemispheres.

In examining Rudolf Steiner's original board drawing relating to this lecture, it struck me that it gives the child an example of an 'almost complete idea:' the right side of the form, which requires completing in line with the other half, already contains a part of the whole form, so that it becomes easier for the child to draw the remainder (*see* drawing).

As additional integration training for the collaboration of both hemispheres, Vera Birkenbihl recommends using laterality crossover exercises, which she largely derives from exercises used in applied kinesiology.[180] These have interesting parallels with an exercise mentioned by Rudolf Steiner directly following his comments on mirrored forms:

Then one can also continue by getting the children to develop skills in tangible, pictorial thinking: 'Point to your right eye with your left hand ... Point to your right eye with your right hand ... Point from behind to your left shoulder with your right hand ... Now your right shoulder with your left hand ... Point to your left ear with your right hand ... Point to your left ear with your left hand ... Point to your right big toe with your right hand ... etc.

In other words, get the children to accomplish all sorts of odd exercises relating to their own body. For example, also: Draw a circle with your right hand round your left hand ... Draw a circle with your left hand round your right ... Draw two circles which your hands form inside each other ... Draw two circles at once with both hands, one on one side, the other on the other ...

Get them to do this with increasing speed: Move the middle finger of your right hand quickly! Move the thumb of your right hand quickly! Move your little finger quickly! Thus you get the child to perform all kinds of exercises with swift presence of mind.

What is the effect of such exercises? If a child does these around the age of eight, they will learn to think, for life.[181]

Steiner's guidelines are often regarded as spatial orientation exercises, and already used with children in Class One (age six/seven) to consolidate their awareness of left and right.[182] In fact, Steiner himself only mentions them in connection with mirrored forms 'around the age of eight.'

Rudolf Steiner's aim here, he states, is nothing more nor less than to nurture children's skills in pictorial thinking with the aid of the body. Why then (as Dühnfort/Kranich suggest) should the teacher do these exercises (where necessary even the other way round) at the same time as pupils, simultaneously speaking the instruction words?

In my view, Steiner's recommendations are optimum exercises for integration of the two sides of the brain. My experience with a fifteen-year-old dyslexic while working through the alphabet (see p. 80) suggests that the verbally issued direction ('Point to ... = L mode) should be linked with a picture (left ear, right shoulder, big toe = R mode). In this case, performing the bodily movement itself would reinforce the connection (as is the case in kinesiology). In these activities 'putting oneself in the picture,' which Steiner consistently urges or demonstrates, again occurs. (see pp. 115–18, 121, 152).

Rudolf Steiner likewise envisages such exercises for children presented to him as 'delayed in school development' (maybe dyslexics?) or inattentive children (perhaps ADD?).

'Attentiveness' in itself is for Steiner no criterion for the capacity to observe and learn. He says, 'It's said that we can teach a child something when he pays attention — attention to what he may then forget again quite soon ...'[183] Instead, Steiner gets such children to first do crossover, picturing and symmetry exercises, in order then to diagnose 'slow' or 'quick' gifts.

Since the described exercise for 'tangible, pictorial thinking' is also used by Steiner as a diagnosis exercise, I wondered whether there might be parallels here with Ronald Davis's perceptual ability assessment exercise. In this, the student is asked to imagine a piece of cake on the flat of his hand, and then to place his 'mind's eye' into the index finger of the other hand. The counsellor guides the person's index finger around the 'cake' and gets him/her to describe it from different perspectives. [184]

I got a fourteen-year-old dyslexic who had just learned the Davis method to do Steiner's 'picture-thinking' exercise, and then asked her what she had 'seen' and felt. She found it fun to observe herself in zigzag alternation from many sides. When I asked her to compare it with the 'cake exercise' she said it was similar: 'In one, I looked at cake, in the other, myself.'

Whereas kinesiology movement sequences (Birkenbihl) can quickly lead to mechanical or automatic movements, Steiner's exercises always require the child's full attention (L + R mode), and the continual change of task and increasing tempo train integration of both hemispheres still more.

But if a teacher joined in with the exercises (and even did them reversed) I think this would firstly confuse the children in their own activity, and secondly, induce them to follow the teacher's movements in a kind of gymnastics. In so doing, there would be no need for the children to invoke their own pictures in relation to the movement sequences, and they would no longer be 'in the picture' themselves. Steiner therefore explicitly requires these exercises to be ones where children 'make movements in which one must reflect, then later on one will become adept at life ...' [185]

I believe one should consider this if using Steiner's exercises in class — something I would very much recommend:

It always has a certain effect on the child when one tries to start from pictures, but pictures which connect with their own corporeal nature, their own bodies; in other words, one shouldn't start from some pictorial element that the child merely observes, that is outside him, but from the picture of touching your lower left arm with your right hand, or suchlike. This pictorial quality, in which the child must put himself in the picture, is something that has a continuous effect on him.[186]

Food for Thought

In the *Frankfurter Rundschau* on November 15, 1997, author Peter Wirtz wrote:

The brain sees the future
A period of 50 milliseconds intervenes between a ray of light arriving on the eye's retina and the response of the brain's visual centre. During this time a moving object has already changed its position again. Our brain therefore perceives a condition that already lies in the past.

The human brain performs an astonishing number of calculations related to sense impressions. For instance, a vertical measure appears markedly longer than a horizontal one. Our brain does not show us the actual world but a distorted picture of it. This censoring of reality probably arose during evolution to increase survival probability.

Romi Nijhawan, of Cornell University's Psychology Institute in Ithaca, USA, has been able to demonstrate that our brain is also involved in dynamic calculations while perceiving moving objects. We see a state that is 50 milliseconds in the past, but our brain extrapolates from the movement the, literally, provisional location of the object. Thanks to such calculations we usually therefore see the object where it actually is. Romi Nijhawan accurately calls this process 'predictive perception.'

The following passage comes from the oldest known description of Mohammed's life, by Ibn Ishaq, and was written around 120 years after the prophet died:

The dream vision
Each year Mohammed withdrew into isolation to the mountain of Hira. Thus too did he in the year that he became forty. Then came the night which was to be the holiest of his life, the night of Al-Kadr.

As I was sleeping, the prophet later related, the angel Gabriel came to me with a cloth of brocade, upon which something was written, and said, 'Read!'

'I cannot read,' I replied.

Then he pressed the cloth upon me so that I thought it would be my death. Then he let me go and said once more, 'Read!'

'I cannot read,' I replied.

And again he suffocated me with the cloth, so that I thought I would die. And when he released me he said again, 'Read!'

And for the third time I replied, 'I cannot read!'

At that he again suffocated me almost to death and ordered me once again to read. And, in fear he might so treat me again, I asked, 'What should I read?'

Then he said, 'Read, in the name of thy Lord, who creates, creates man from congealed blood! Read, for thy Lord is most generous! Who taught the pen! Taught man what he did not know!' [187]

I repeated these words, and as I ended, he went away from me. But I awoke and it seemed to me as though the words were inscribed in my heart ...

By S. Aurobindo, Indian yoga practitioner and philosopher (1910):

The intellect is an organ composed of several groups of functions, divisible into two important classes, the functions and faculties of the right-hand, the functions and faculties of the left-hand.

The faculties of the right-hand are comprehensive, creative and synthetic; the faculties of the left-hand critical and analytic ... The left-hand touches only the body of knowledge, the right-hand penetrates its soul. The left-hand limits itself to ascertained truth, the right-hand grasps that which is still elusive or unascertained. Both are essential to the completeness of the human reason.

These important functions of the human being have all to be raised to their highest and finest working-power if the education of the child is not to be imperfect and one-sided.

Johann Wolfgang Goethe on his 'cardinal error:'

I never cared to learn the craft of a subject which I wanted or was supposed to pursue ... either it was compelled by the power of the mind, and succeeded or failed; or, if I desired to accomplish something well and with consideration, I was fearful, and was unable to complete it.

The other, closely related error is that I never wished to spend so much time upon any work or matter as it would require.

Since I have the good fortune to be able to think and combine a very great deal in a short space of time, accomplishing something in gradual stages is boring and unendurable for me.

To End With (not an Afterword)

A proper book — one might think — not only needs a proper foreword, but also a proper afterword to end with: perhaps a summary or summation, a concluding overview of the most salient points. However, this book has no desire to round things off and conclude them, but would much prefer to leave everything wide open; and so I prefer to write another foreword to end with. There is naturally no end to the book's themes and issues, its problems, questions and hopes. When you close this book after a few further pages, I hope this will only be the beginning.

Please do not therefore regard my ideas on the acquisition of literacy skills — where I've been able to put them down in any ordered or comprehensible way — as 'final truths.' For me, too many of these things are still purely theoretical findings. Practical trials and experiences over long periods, involving large numbers of cases, may confirm one or another of these ideas, or else perhaps also reveal them to be illusory. At any rate, ongoing, lively and dynamic mutual learning is needed. I hope this book will stimulate you in this direction, even if it has sometimes provoked you. It was never going to be an easy ride. And it was always going to be just a beginning.

In reading Rudolf Steiner's lectures on education, I repeatedly find parallels and connections that would need further research. For instance, comparative studies would be needed between Steiner's comments on maths teaching and the Davis method for tackling numeracy difficulties (being able to count is the basis for both), or with the learning strategies devised by Barbara Meister Vitale to nurture maths skills in right-hemisphere children (starting from the whole).

More detailed work also needs to be done on the connections (which to my mind are evident) between Steiner's recommendations for foreign-language teaching and attempts to use the findings of brain research in foreign-language acquisition.[188]

Here, though, special note should be taken of Rudolf Steiner's comment on the transition from oral foreign-language teaching to written use of a foreign language: 'In foreign language teaching, too, one needs to arrive at reading via writing first.'[189]

In relation to all questions which at present remain unanswered, however, I'd like to place special emphasis on the following appeal: use of the Davis method in schools must be developed further. For all children! DDA institutes in the UK and US offer regular training and workshop sessions for teachers (*see* contact details on p.179).

For all children — not just those who are clearly dyslexic, and especially those who seem indefinably 'difficult' and who in increasing numbers are proclaimed to have so-called 'attention deficit disorders' — this kind of holistic learning is a real, realizable utopia which I believe in.

Henning Köhler says there is no such thing as a 'difficult child.' The truth may be that we are making things too difficult for them and ourselves. It may be that our world needs this bombardment of perceptions and influx of chaos, which may be directing the way into and through the coming millennia. Such a thought is not unfounded. Jean Gebser, for instance, has authored some fascinating philosophical observations on a forthcoming (or already begun?) age of 'aperspective.' His descriptions of a more holistic type of perception and emancipation from logical time are surely reminiscent of the 'gift of disorientation.'

The field of science, too, is supplying us with many potentially interesting connections and explanations, such as biochemist and cellular biologist Rupert Sheldrake's model for explaining processes by which forms arise in nature. This goes far beyond what brain research has told us so far. He posits truly exciting hypotheses about the causes of form creation, for instance, that all natural forms are determined by formative (morphogenetic) fields which as it were represent 'nature's memory' since they store all the 'experiences' of all individuals of a species — whether crystals, plants, animals or humans. If this is true, then multi-level, intuitive, pictorial thinking may also be a special gift for communicating with these formative 'fields.'

Brain research will likewise provide many new findings in the future, even if some of it still currently remains unexplained and contradictory — as one can see, for instance, from continually updated commentaries by Springer/Deutsch. Nevertheless, I think we can learn a great deal by linking statements from people who think 'differently' from the norm (whether they are geniuses from the past such as Rudolf Steiner or modern lateral thinkers like Barbara Meister Vitale, Vera Birkenbihl or Ronald Davis). By combining their intuitive thinking and grasp of connections with further scientific and logical discoveries we can all gain a new perspective and increased respect for the potential capacities in each person.

To finish, let me return to the gift, described in Part I, which according to Davis underlies dyslexia. Pictorial, felt thinking and the disorientation function lead to a capacity for non-verbal conceptualization and to 'mastery.' For me, as a predominantly verbal thinker, it was initially very difficult to understand the process of non-verbal conceptualization. Ronald Davis's findings, my practical work with dyslexic children and teenagers, and above all my reading of Rudolf Steiner's lectures and books, helped me a great deal. Often in this process, the pieces of the jigsaw put themselves together — as in the following circumstances, which once again reveal the feeling, pictorial thinking mode of those involved, and give us a hint of what 'mastery' means.

I was in the process of working through the basis of symbol mastery with Rebeca (age 10). To help her understand that complete mastery of a word involves knowing its sound and way of writing it, I asked her to create a fantasy word: she was to invent something that doesn't exist, and then give this creation a name. Thus she created the 'duckcatfantbird' animal.

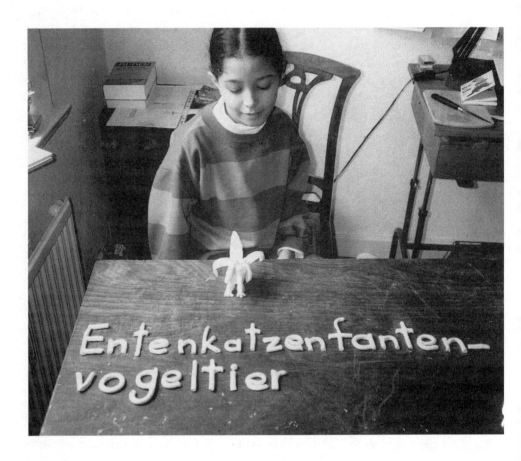

She hummed happily as she worked: 'I'm creating, I'm creating.' A little while later — after we'd talked about the meaning of her creature, and its name, and clarified that anyone who heard this word would know what it was, or that anyone who saw the animal could only talk about it with us if he also knew the word for it — she began to murmur to herself, as though lost in a dream, 'Whoever grasps the sense of speech, to him the world in images reveals itself ...'

I was very struck and asked her how she knew this verse. Then she told me that her class had to say it every morning in their current main lesson on grammar. Two days later, I encountered the verse again — this time all of it — when I looked at Rebeca's main lesson book to see how her handwriting was progressing. I had to smile when I saw the author's name at the bottom.

Language

1. Whoever grasps the sense of speech,
    to him the world in images
    reveals itself;

2. Whoever hears the soul of speech,
    to him the world as being
    opens itself;

3. Whoever experiences the spirit of speech,
    to him the world gives
    the power of wisdom;

4. Whoever comes to love speech,
    will be endowed
    by speech itself with its own power.

5. And so I'll turn my heart and aim
    to word's spirit and soul;

6. And with love for it feel
    myself, at last, entire.

Rudolf Steiner

I wrote it down and gave it to two sixteen-year-old picture thinkers (whom I call 'A' and 'B' below). At the same time, I gave them each (separately) the following task and recorded their spontaneous associations in relation to it (which was quite difficult, since I couldn't easily keep pace with what they were saying):

'Please read to the end of each verse and then tell me what you see or feel (corresponding to the third stage of learning to read: the aim, in line with Davis, being full understanding of what has been read).

Verse 1: A: It's about someone who responds properly to what is said. If you don't do that in images, you won't understand the words.	B: Educated people who have a lot to do with language and grasp it. The fact that all becomes clear. A flow of images; enlightenment.
Verse 2: A: If you understand the speaker, the picture comes to life.	B: Comes alive.
Verse 3: A: If you experience what's spoken in images, you discover things that others don't, or don't see in the same way.	B: A soul passes through the head, through the mouth; words fall, everything accumulates in the brain. Old, wise people. Ancient China. You gain wisdom.
Verse 4: A: Whoever can use it well creates power.	B: Spoken love poem. Upsurge of power. One is filled by it. You get something from it, learn something new.
Verse 5: A: Give free rein; say what you think.	B: Someone who gives talks, preaches. Using language.
Verse 6: A: If you can do all this, the word becomes an 'I,' a connection is formed, you master the word.	B: Spring. Poems. People in harmony.

Maybe this is a vision of the future, this perfect communication where the 'I' enters into connection with the word and 'masters' it, where poetry finds its true space and people live in harmony ... maybe.

Appendices

I. Samples of Dyslexics' Writing — a Different View

Below are samples of text written by nine dyslexics aged between eight and sixteen. All currently attend a Waldorf school, and four previously attended a mainstream school. Five of them previously participated in one or more series of therapy.

All show one or more kinds of 'disorder' (or the effect of the disorientation mode). These range from delayed language development, sound discrimination problems, articulation disorders (hazy speech, stuttering, lisping), acoustic and/or visual perception disturbances (many have a pair of glasses at home which they don't use), disorders of the sense of balance, movement and/or time, behavioural issues related to attention (ADD, ADHD), and numeracy problems, through to school stress and school refusal. Their abilities in reading and writing vary, although all started from a low level.

All of them are right-handed, though compounded by much ambidexterity and sometimes crossed dominance. In at least five cases, other family members are also dyslexic.

The sentences, short stories, texts and poems have mostly arisen following work on a trigger word tackled through symbol mastery (in line with the book by Ronald Davis). This also explains their somewhat odd titles. Some titles arose from other contexts ('The Mushrooom,' 'Recycling'). The texts by teenagers printed elsewhere in this book (see p.128) were mostly stimulated by the book *Learning to Write Without a Doubt (Garantiert schreiben lernen)*.

Apart from the idea furnished by the title, nothing else was suggested in advance. My involvement in these 'works' extended only to correcting the spelling and punctuation.

The texts accurately reflect their authors' holistic mode of thinking (and do so increasingly as they get older): pictorial language, complete ideas, humour, multi-layered perceptions and a perspective that may sometimes seem paradoxical, along with a strong gift for observation. One finds precisely formulated perceptions but scarcely any linear sequence of 'and then … and then … and then' that is otherwise so common in school essays.

These texts also give us insights into their authors' world of feeling and experience, especially in relation to their experiences with reading, writing and school in general.[*]

Ricarda (8/9)

In
The duck sits in the nest and on the branch is a nest and in the nest is a bird, for it's evening and night is coming

To
At last school is over. Frank's dad is already standing by the car, because I'm going to Frank's house today. Once we've eaten lunch we are going to go riding.

Then
Hans says, 'Lisa, it's my go on the swing!'
'No,' says Lisa.
Then the mother comes. 'Lisa, go and play in the sandpit!' Lisa cries.
Then her father comes and says, 'Lisa, we're going for a walk with Leo.'

On
'Frank, do you know where my glasses are?'
'What did you say, granddad?'
'Do you know where my glasses are?
'Yes, on your nose!'

Us
Frank and Lisa have baked a cake. They made it with chocolate. They put it on the table to cool down. When they come back they see Hans breaking off a big piece of Frank's and Lisa's cake. 'Hey, that cake belongs to us!'

---

[*]   Translator's note: the 'title' words do not always appear as frequently in the texts themselves, due to differences of preposition use between English and German. The rhymed versions of poems given in the original are inevitably approximations only.

„Franzi weißt du, wo meine Brille ist?
„Was hast du gesagt Opa?" „Weißt du, wo
meine Brille ist? „Ja, **auf** deiner Nase.

Rebeca (10)

To

Once upon a time there was a To who sometimes lived here, and at other times there. One day the To went to the sea. It washed and brushed its o. Then it went home. So ended the story of To.

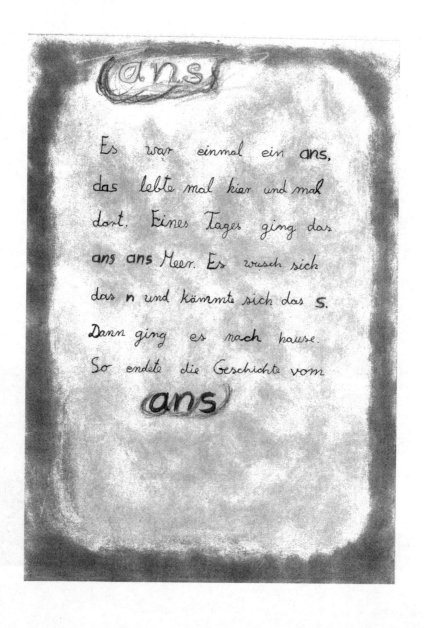

Farina (11)

Nothing
I sit at my desk and
I have nothing *to write.*
That's why I didn't
want to write the word nothing!

He
He is very sweet, little Max

There
'There with the moon I stand and gaze down!'

Farina Engel   11,2, 99

„Dort beim Mond ♥ steh' ich und kuck runter!"

Franzi (11)

The Mushroom

You mushroom, you odd creature.
You're almost only in shade
and sometimes in light.
And you need hardly any water
though others need it indeed.
From others you draw
your food and your strength.
You live on tree and plant,
although they're green no longer.
They've dried out completely
in the cold mushroom forest.
And yet you're the favourite food
of snails and slugs and flies.
You stand there all alone
with children and with wife.
You mushroom, you odd creature.

Maro (13)

Want

Two hedgehogs, both so spiky-fine
Want to cross the river Rhine.
The river looks so deep and wide
They build a raft to get to the other side.

Here there's quite a lot of wood.
The raft is built. It does look good!
Rhine's other side is not so far.
They can make it, they are sure.

Shortly before the further bank
The great Lord Hedgehog rears his flank
And says, 'What is it you want here?'
They call back: 'We're delivering beer!'

The Lord says, 'Welcome, come to lunch!'
For somehow he liked them very much.
They landed on the bank and there
He chased them off again and took the
beer.

This Lord was really very dumb:
The barrel held no beer, no rum.
The hedgehogs laughed aloud, for see
The barrel was entirely empty.

Out

Out of the house
Runs Mrs Mouse
To Mrs Frowze.
Mouse laughs loud
At Mrs Frowze
For Mrs Frowze
Hates the mouse
And Mrs Frowze
Goes berserk, cries out:
'Oh no, the mouse
is in my house.
That lout of a mouse —
Get out, get out!

He and It

One day Gregory saw the
stinkbeast in the wood. It turned
round and saw him. He stopped
still and was afraid of it. He
wanted to creep away quietly. It
noticed this, though, and ran up
to him. It lifted its tail. He said,
'Pooh, it stinks!' Then it said,
'Well leave me in peace then!'

And he ran away .

Yes

This yes it's evident
Is an important word.
So let's see what is meant:
You can use it as a question,
For example if you ask:
'Must I really do this task?'
'Must I really do it, yes?'
A very important word
But it's said so very quickly —
Just like that
And yet, and yet:
Trying to explain it
Is enough to make you gasp.
Don't you think it's wonderful
My little poem about yes?

Answer: ...

From

From this day on he swore:
'Sweet things I will eat no more.'

For yesterday he won
A box of chocolates from Kingston.
They sent it to his home in Seaton
And immediately they were eaten!
In the night he felt so ill.
His mother thought: 'That serves him right.'
Next morning when his waking bell
Rang out, he really wasn't well.
His friends from school said, 'Have a sweet ...'
But nothing would ever make him eat
A sweet again for quite a while.

From this day on he swore:
'Sweet things I will eat no more.'

Jenny (14)

Me
When I came into class today, I found a love letter under my seat, and it said: 'I love you, yours ...' I wrote below it: 'I love me too' and I hung the note up on the wall. That's because I didn't know who wrote it, so I couldn't return it to him.

How
Pedro went to the Pope. 'Good morning, Mr Pope,' said Pedro.
'How dare you speak to me like that?' said the Pope. 'Off to the dungeon, I don't want to see you any more!'
So Pedro sat in the dungeon and made a hat out of a piece of paper — a beautiful hat.
When the guards saw the hat they took a step back in amazement. 'My God, how beautiful that hat is,' they said. The guards went to the Pope and told him about the hat. The Pope wanted to see it immediately.
When he arrived in the dungeon there was no hat to be seen.
'How can that be?' cried the guards together. 'The hat was just here a moment ago!'
On the ground lay nothing but a bit of crumpled paper.
Pedro, sitting in the corner, jumped up and said, 'I can do magic!' 'What? How?' said the Pope. 'Simply like this,' said Pedro and clicked his fingers. 'Simply like that?' repeated the Pope in amazement. 'Yes, simply like that. I can show you. I can make myself invisible.' 'Invisible?' echoed the others, astonished. 'You can do that?' 'Sure, but you must all look away for a moment!'
The guards and the Pope all shut their eyes. Pedro slipped very, very quietly away, and was never ever seen again.

Max (16)

Boring
'Things that aren't fresh any more all taste old and stale,' said Tomec as Steffi was just sampling a little bit of cheese.
'Yuck, you're right,' she said, spitting out half the cheese again.
'Let's cook something instead.'
'OK, but only if you bring the food with you.'
'Good. See you!'
CLICK!

Looking/seeing
The light was shining through the blinds. I was sitting in front of my old black-and-white TV set again, gazing at the flickering screen as though enchanted.
It was a nature documentary about tropical and subtropical birds of prey.

I was particularly interested in the eagle — and had been since last year's bird expedition in the summer. But I only have a couple of overexposed colour pictures that are so great visually that you can only see them through glasses or contact lenses.

Suddenly!!! a ray of light streamed through the blinds and blinded me!

Gerrit (16)

The sea
The sea is calm.
The boat is reflected in the water.
Wind rises.
The boat rocks.
The waves grow bigger.
The water foams.
The waves crash onto the deck.
It grows dark.
The sea is wild.

It begins to rain.
It is cold.
Lightning flashes.
The deck is wet.
The lightning reflects in the waterdrops.
The sea is wild.

The winds drop.
The sea is calm.
The boat is reflected in the water.

Junge (18, Cape Town)

Fear is all Around
I find that in the 21st century, probably the most feared thing is — being judged or being left out.

So many people go through pain and fear of rejection.

To fit somewhere you have to smoke or take drugs in order to be accepted. Otherwise you are afraid of being on your own; this is when you are lost in your own world.

You are afraid of failing in school and you feel you failed your friends and family.

There are many things which seem to be foolish, but some of us are afraid of things such as: commitment to love and marriage, heights, animals or even being in front of a crowd.

Some of us are afraid of even not succeeding in our dreams.
I think the greatest fear of all is not living life at its fullest.

Junge, 18

And finally, a collage of handwriting samples from the same children and teenagers:

II. Further Information on the Davis Method

Contact details

For the Davis Dyslexia Association (DDA) in Ireland and the UK:
Davis Learning Foundation
Licensed affiliate of Davis Dyslexia Association International
PO Box 972
Canterbury
Kent CT1 9DN
Tel: +44 (0)1227 732288
Fax: +44 (0)1227 731756
Website: www.davislearningfoundation.org.uk
Email: info@davislearningfoundation.org.uk

In the USA:
Davis Learning Strategies
1601 Bayshore Highway,
Suite 260,
Burlingame, CA 94010
Tel: +1 650 6927141 or +1 888 8057216
Fax: +1 650 692 7075
Website: www.davislearn.com
Email: info@davislearn.com

DDA international:
Website: www.dyslexia.com
email: ddai@dyslexia.com
Training: training@dyslexia.com

In line with DDA international, the Davis Learning Foundation pursues the goal of encouraging better awareness of:
- what dyslexia is, and associated learning styles;
- the gifts that accompany it;
- how aspects detrimental to learning can be overcome.

Continually updated contact details for certified Davis counsellors can be found on the Internet, or requested from the Davis Learning Foundation, which also issues a free regular e-newsletter

Literature on the Davis method

See bibliography listings for: Davis, Ronald D.; Temple, Robin; Steltzer, Saskia.

Some case histories using the Davis method

Journals published by the DDA-affiliated institutes frequently contain case histories. Drawn from my own experience I would like to add to these:

- A report by a mother who is working with her daughter on Ron Davis's book;
- Interviews with dyslexic pupils;
- An interview with Matthias Gradenwitz, a former Waldorf teacher and today a certified Davis counsellor or facilitator.

First here, is a case history documented by a mother whose daughter has been attending the same class as my own daughter for some time. When she read Ronald Davis's book, she immediately recognized her daughter's characteristics. After discussing it with me, they both decided to work together on the book. That is also how the book was originally conceived. Experience has shown, though, that it is very difficult to work with one's own child, especially if the child has already undergone various therapeutic interventions, and continually regards herself as defective. In their case, however, it seemed to work. I asked them to record their experiences.

Svenja, February 1999

My daughter and I had a very good connection with each other from the beginning. As our life continued this connection intensified so that when we were apart we knew how the other was. Telephone calls were often unnecessary. I don't mention this to wrap us in some kind of mysterious aura. It was or is a quite normal condition for us. Unfortunately there was one problem: Svenja had enormous difficulties with reading and writing. Somehow or other, with much exertion, she managed to cope at school. Her problems were made worse by the fact that her mother tongue is German but she started school abroad. She attended school in Copenhagen for four years, then went to the international school in Class Five and Six (ages 11/12) and now attends Class Seven at a Rudolf Steiner school. She learned English and Danish very quickly, but her problems with reading and writing continued. She was always very conscientious about trying to write, but often whatever she learned laboriously one day had gone the next. On the other hand, she had gifts which were far ahead of her age group.

I never found fault with her for not being able to read and write properly. We both tried to do whatever was possible. She picked up lots of little tricks to hide her difficulties.

In her present class the teacher told us about a method which draws on the 'gifts' of dyslexics, presented in the book by Ronald Davis. After picking up this book I couldn't put it down. Since I have always been interested in philosophies that regard it as normal for people to have out-of-body perceptions, and have also experienced this in relation to my daughter, the puzzle of Svenja's reading problems started to make sense.

I had a session with Frau Jantzen, who herself has experienced the sufferings of dyslexic children. She uses the Davis method to help such children. After a very interesting conversation, my daughter and I decided that I myself would accompany my daughter through this programme.

Day 1

I first familiarized myself with the method by studying the book carefully. We then carried out the first step (perceptual ability assessment) and my daughter found that she could perceive her surroundings from all possible perspectives. When I saw this I was astonished. She simply said that this was normal for her.

For instance, on the same day we went to the riding stables and sat down by the riding track. She said, 'You know, it's completely normal for me to be able to look from where I am, or instead from the rider's view, and I never knew that other people can't do this.'

She herself only now became aware of this gift, which is one of the talents normal for dyslexics. As far as I am concerned these are real perceptions, since the human being is a spiritual being within a body. We can call it soul or something else — whatever you like. In this context, though, only dyslexics seem to have this faculty for perceiving outside their body in this way.

After this first session we knew, therefore, that Svenja is dyslexic, and this was a powerful experience for us. In relation to written text, for the first time in her life she found a way of looking at things that precisely matched her own experience, e.g. seeing letters from all directions, the appearance of script as if it is all a single entity etc.

Day 2

Today we had to take a step which gave Svenja a means to see the letters through her eyes alone and not from all directions, which naturally shows letters in an incredible variety of positions (orientation training).

We accomplished this: Svenja was able to follow all the directions very well. After we had established the orientation point, we ran up against a big problem, for Svenja thought that she must see physically from that point. After clearing up this misunderstanding, she could control the place between her two hemispheres from this point. Then the next problem arose. She began to cry and could no longer find her 'mind's eye.' For the first time she was looking consciously through her eyes at the letters. Then we clarified once again that she didn't have to give up her way of seeing things, but just use the orientation point when she reads, in the same way that I wear glasses. She should just use the point above the back of her head to orientate herself while reading.

It was like a miracle: when Svenja found this point, she could read much better than before, and she noticed immediately if she wasn't focused on this point.

We took a break and started to model the capital alphabet. Every letter that had been problematic for her previously gave rise to specific phenomena, which we handled in line with the recommended steps.

Then another miracle occurred. After going through the alphabet five times to iron out any misunderstandings, Svenja was able to recite the alphabet backwards by heart, easily and fluently. This seemed incredible to me, since I myself couldn't have done it at that speed. Yet this was not all: I could give her any letter of the alphabet and, without hesitation, she could tell me the preceding and following letter by heart. I can simply say that I can't do this, and I think any 'normal' person would certainly need some time to be able to do it. I believe that one should consider what 'normal' actually means: corresponding to the norm. This gift exceeds that.

After Svenja saw that she herself had achieved this, and that I couldn't do it as fast as her, she was overjoyed.

I believe that this was the first time in her life that she knew she had a chance of learning to read and write.

Day 3

On day three, we worked through the lower case alphabet. Whenever Svenja was confused we checked the orientation point, or found additional misunderstandings relating to letters. By and large things flowed much better, and Svenja was enthusiastically engaged. We then also worked on punctuation, and Svenja finished the day in good spirits.

We are now working on clarifying the main trigger words, after I worked through a great deal of grammar with her.

During this work Svenja decided that I should write down everything relating to grammar, or other things that we encountered, to help others who have the same problems as Svenja. I am now using this method with Svenja in every school subject. We clarify the words, model concepts that cause misunderstanding, until she gets it. Svenja's handwriting has got much better. The teacher told me that there are clear signs of success. Svenja is now managing her homework much better, and mostly does it on her own.

I find it remarkable that Mr Davis developed this method, and would like to express my gratitude.

A.K.

Interviews with pupils

In the following interviews I asked pupils questions individually and initially recorded their answers on tape. The children and teenagers involved were the same ones who wrote the sample texts already quoted.

C.J.: *You are dyslexic. How and when do you notice that?*

Ricarda: Because I can't do maths so well, nor write very well. Sometimes, when I have to find my point, I'm always so fidgety.

Max: At school, in lessons.

Jenny: When I'm reading or writing

Gerrit: Since Class One, when I started with reading. I didn't know what dyslexia is, I just couldn't read, but it didn't bother me.

Maro: When I'm writing and reading. If I have to read out loud, I don't manage it, and everyone stares at me. Before, when it wasn't clear I was dyslexic, everyone used to think that I was stupid or something. In my confirmation group you sometimes have to read aloud. When I read so hesitantly, they all laugh sometimes.

C.J.: *How does your mother/your parents handle it or respond?*

R: She understands. Just sometimes, when I'm so fidgety she says, 'Find your point!' and then I say, 'No, I'm having a break, I don't want to right now.'

Max: With understanding.

J: They send me to you. They're willing to help me a lot with my homework. They are understanding. If I need something I can always ask them.

G: Well, they just leave me in peace.

M: They have understanding for it. If I forget something, like the date, my mother says, 'It's OK, you're not so with it right now.'

C.J.: How did and do your teachers handle it?

R: In my old school the teacher tore up my work. Because it was all wrong. In my new school it's good now.

Max: It used to be a bit of a problem, but now — yes, it's pretty OK. My new school is more aware of it.

J: In primary school the teacher often got me to read to her at break times. Then in Classes Five to Seven [age 11–13] I didn't get any more help; the teachers just treated me normally. And now, in Class Eight [age 14], the teacher is very understanding if I don't get something. But maybe that's not so good because the others realize, and that's also crap.

G: They never really said anything; they never said I had to do it, never put any pressure on me.

M: Well, with ... (class teacher) things are better now; it's changed. The other teachers, I don't even know if they're aware of it. Things are just the same as they used to be in foreign languages.

C.J.: You now know how the Davis method works, with orientation and symbol mastery. Many people can't properly imagine what it means to be orientated, in other words to find the point with your mind's eye. What does this mean for you?

R: When I go to my point, I am always calmer and more focused.

Max: This is not being 'concentrated' but rather one can adjust to something, approach it, but one doesn't concentrate on it.

J: I simply imagine that the point is there, and then I go to it, and then I begin to read, and think no more about it. It's become automatic now: when I read I orientate myself. I no longer really notice the difference.

G: It's just different. When I'm reading, if I concentrate too hard on it, it's chaos; but if I go gently to the point, then it works.

M: When I'm there I'm also more focused. I can better concentrate on what's written in front of me, everything is easier. Things are more relaxed.

C.J.: What is it like, in contrast, if you're disorientated while reading or writing, and leave the point?

R: Then I'm really fidgety and don't get much done, and also write a lot of things wrong. I don't notice this so much when I'm reading — I can read much better now.

Max: Well, the letters start flying about when I'm away from my point. Everything, which is then outside my field of vision, it all goes in different directions, shifts position. I can't see it all properly any more. I just see one point on the sheet of paper.

J: Then they're stupid letters which flutter about. Then suddenly everything gets confused. You overlook a word and hop to a lower line, make mistakes, lose your place, read a word that has a similar sound and things like that.

G: Just a whole load of signs, no distance any more, and they just look like hieroglyphs.

M: Then a word suddenly comes and I'm out of it, and then the whole thing comes back again. Sometimes I read the word many times but then I somehow read it wrong, leaving out a letter and not seeing it.

C.J.: Dyslexics largely think in pictures and feelings, and do so at a speed that can scarcely be consciously perceived. How is that for you? Let's take a word as an example: what do you see or feel with the word 'lion?'

R: What do I see? Well, I see a lion in the desert under some funny-looking trees, with a kind of very flat, broad crown. Then I also see a herd of gnus.

Max: Animal, no, king of the jungle. All sorts of pictures.

J: I see a lion who stands there strong and big with his great mane, who walks and displays his strength, who roars. If I think further about it, I can imagine how he runs, leaps, how he lies, how he sleeps. I've just seen him running through the Sahara. It all happens so quickly you can't say it all.

G: Strength, cry ... roar ... well, the character of a lion. His character remains whether he lies there, or attacks someone, or doesn't. In different roles: when he's lying, leaping, running. It's simply there.

M: *Yellow, in other words: lion with mane and so on, with mouth open, and around him the savannah, a couple of trees and grass. Yes, he can move too, then he goes, and in the background are other animals, and then he lies down.*

C.J.: Some words have no direct pictorial meaning, e.g. little words like 'when,' or 'in case'... Then we work on them using the definitions in the dictionary, and also usually model the term in clay. How did you find this?

R: *It makes everything go better. When I model, I write the words more correctly afterwards.*

Max: *Yes, I can remember many things better because this makes the word stick, so that I rarely forget it again.*

J: *Yes, when I read. The words I know, I read, and then I'm not even aware that I couldn't read them the last time. I'm not exactly sure whether I can do it better because I modelled the letters, or because I'm simply reading more now. But when I read you sometimes notice it, and then you say it, and I remember that I did model that word.*

G: *Really only positive experiences. To begin with I didn't believe that it would help at all, I thought it was a bit silly really. But it does help.*

M: *Just good experiences, I'd say. It does help me progress. For example, 'the' and 'it' and so on — it's not so confusing now.*

C.J.:You have written some of your own texts or poems. How did you find that?

R: *Writing stories is good. And then you also get the words much better, if you've written something yourself, and then I can also keep it better in my head.*

Max: *Was great fun, was a laugh, often.*

J: *I enjoyed doing it. It's also very helpful to fix the word you've just modelled, as it were; to imagine all the situations in which the word occurs.*

G: *Yes, I was astonished that I was able to do it. Some people were really taken with the poems.*

M: *It was fun. Beforehand I wasn't really sure I could do it.*

C.J.: Ronald Davis says that for most dyslexics the word 'school' can best be described as 'frustration.' How is that for you?

R: *Yes, school is simply stupid. It's got a bit better.*

Max: Yes — yes, yes, yes, yes, yes, yes, yes, yes, yes, yes — yes, yes!

J: Yes, yes, definitely.
G: Um, I don't really think that's true — I've never really had pressure put on me, and so I always go (to school) — but yes, OK — shit — but it has to be done, and somehow I manage now.

M: Yes, if I think about school, for instance, in the holidays, I feel frustrated, and get into a bad mood.

C.J.: Is there anything you'd like to say to teachers who have dyslexics in their classes?

R: Well, yes, maybe that they shouldn't get so uptight if one hasn't done enough work.

Max: Um — no, I don't know. Many teachers are already pretty good — well, maybe not many, but ... they should have understanding for the pupils, for their work.

J: Mm. Well I think dyslexics don't really need these extra sessions. We're not stupid or anything. They should be able to ask if they haven't understood something. The lessons should simply make space for that.

G: Um, well, do history chronologically, not always jumping about. But of course you can't always do that.

M: Yes, that they should somehow be more aware of it, and take things a bit more slowly. When they've put writing on the board, they shouldn't wipe the board immediately. And with reading, they could wait a bit every now and then.

C.J.: Is there anything you'd like to say to other dyslexics and/or to their parents?

R: Don't know — that they shouldn't be sad; it also has its good aspects. And that everyone, the whole world, should do modelling.

M: Nothing to be said about that.

J: Don't put yourself under so much pressure; it won't do any good. Then you might do a test really well one week, but a week later you've forgotten it all. That's no good. For me, the Davis method is better, but I can't be sure that it would be for everyone.

G: What should I say to them? Well, the therapy I had in the past, for two years ... it was useless, and I was pretty frustrated by it. I knew from the start that it wouldn't help. What did I learn there? The paired series and the vowels but nothing more. Reading was one long catastrophe in therapy, and sometimes I started to cry. I wasn't meant to guess but to read. It was pretty frustrating. There was more pressure on me there than at school. And then, with the Davis method, I was sceptical, but it helped.

M: That they should be more relaxed about it, not get so stressed.

C.J.: Dyslexia is a gift, e.g. the capacity for multi-level perception and fast, pictorial thinking. Are you — from this point of view — pleased to be dyslexic?

R: Yes, but it's also stupid. Why can the others always do everything much better?

Max: Yes. I notice this all the time. In many things, such as thinking and things that relate to life in general. Better at speaking. One event recently brought this home to me, when I was with friends. Sometimes I have this kind of quick insight.

J: Yes, of course.

G: Definitely. I don't know that I notice this directly. I always think the others are taking the piss because of something I've done which they wouldn't have thought of, and for me this is completely normal.

M: Well, maybe. Sometimes I think I'd prefer to be different. But then I discover it's better to be the way I am. You do notice that other kids are different, think differently. Also when you're playing, that they do things quite differently than I would. Completely different strategies.

Interview with Matthias Gradenwitz, certified Davis counsellor

C.J.: Matthias, you have practised many professions; most recently you were a remedial/support teacher at the Michael-Bauer School (Waldorf school with remedial department) in Stuttgart. What inspired you to embark on something new again and become a Davis counsellor?

M.G.: In my work as teacher for children with learning difficulties, there were some things I never fully grasped. When I encountered the Davis method, I started on a train of thought and observations that enabled me to understand how I might really help in such cases. To begin with I was sceptical, and only really became convinced when I tried it out and experienced the success at first-hand. It became clear to me how great a need there is to help children, teenagers and adults in this way.

C.J.: You have now founded your own institute, called ImagoBL, in Bad Nauheim. Why this name?

M.G.: *Its full name is 'ImagoBL Institute for Counselling People Gifted with Dyslexia' (ImagoBL@t-online.de). Pictorial thinking is an important aspect in dyslexics' lives, and thus I chose the name 'imago', meaning picture. 'Counselling people gifted with dyslexia' I chose because, as I see it, dyslexics do not suffer from an illness that needs therapy, but are, rather, gifted people. Counselling and training can show them how to use their capacities and gifts in such a way that they can also read, write and do maths. I looked in the phone book to check how many companies there are with the name 'Imago' and was astonished to find that there were over thirty. So I needed to extend the name 'Imago' in a way that clearly identifies my counselling firm.*

C.J.: At your institute you work along the lines of the Davis method, engaging clients in a thirty-hour basic programme. What do you do specifically?

M.G.: *The thirty-hour basic programme is a standard training method that was developed at the Davis Institute in America, and is used by certified counsellors worldwide. It involves training in various exercise procedures and learning techniques. Most of these procedures are also clearly described in Ronald Davis's book. Firstly' it involves the student learning — if he wishes — to induce an orientated condition in himself, and in this state to intentionally exclude confusion. This process reaches a certain degree of stability in two to three days. Then it's up to the student to learn to use this method as a routine way of dealing with confusion, but he is motivated to do so because he notices that it actually works. He will therefore resort to this technique by preference.*

The second major element in the counselling week is alphabet training through modelling of the letters. In this way he appropriates them in three dimensions and then, with closed eyes, practises imagining what he has modelled so that he can read off the alphabet backwards, from ZYX to A, from his inner picture. In this way it's possible to find out where letters are getting confused, and which ones they are, so that this confusion can be excluded.

The third part of the programme involves us showing the student how he can create images, using clay models, for abstract words that do not have any directly corresponding image in his imagination. At the same time, a parent or helper is involved who can accompany the student in further practice. Once the client has learned these procedures he can, with the aid of the helper, gradually work through three to five hundred words over coming years, and thus effectively exclude the source of confusion.

Another major aspect of the counselling week are the various steps in reading technique, in which the client is shown how, through spelling out initially, and then through targeted use of his pictorial thinking, he can properly absorb reading texts, and reproduce and understand them.

C.J.: What have you experienced in this process?

M.G.: I have been working with this method for about a year now, and have worked with roughly thirty students aged between five and eighteen. For me, one of the most important experiences has been to find that this is a path. Existing problems are not remedied in one go; but those affected do develop trust in themselves, noticing that they are being given effective procedures and processes to overcome their problems. During the counselling week, however, clients repeatedly find that larger contexts dawn on them, as though scales fall from their eyes, giving them access to whole new realms of experience. I have experienced many things that I would not have credited if I had not witnessed them myself. There's little point in describing such things, since I can't expect others to believe them without having experienced them at first-hand. I can only urge people who are affected by these issues — whether as educators or dyslexics — to set to work themselves, for I am certain that they too will experience things they would not otherwise believe.

C.J.: What problems do you encounter in this work?

M.G.: The key question in such developmental processes, the key problem, is that of motivation. How can a student, a child, teenager or adult, kindle in himself the long-term motivation to persist with this process and to develop further?

C.J.: How does counselling continue after this first stage?

M.G.: I mentioned before that a helper or accompanying person plays a major role in continuing the training process, a parent or someone else who goes on working and practising with the client. I maintain regular contact with my clients, and am available to talk to them on the phone or hold additional consultations. In addition, I've begun to establish a weekly modelling workshop, where clients whom I've counselled can participate once a week or once a month in a group session. They can give each other mutual help with working on words, tell each other what they did during the past weeks, and I can support them in this process.

C.J.: What contact do you have with the schools your clients attend?

M.G.: This varies a great deal. There are teachers who sit in on the counselling week to see what we're doing, and who try to integrate and continue it as far as possible in their teaching situation. On the other hand, of course, there are also schools with which I have little or no contact, either because the child doesn't wish it, or because the school isn't interested.

C.J.: Is there anything you'd like to say to teachers who have dyslexics in their class?

M.G.: Yes, of course, there's a lot to say. The most important thing a teacher can do for dyslexics in his class is to form a comprehensive view of how they experience the world.

There are two keys to doing so: one involves unprejudiced observation of how the child is developing, how he approaches things; out of this experience, with insight into the child's strengths, to consider how he (the teacher) can use these strengths for the learning process. The other thing he can do is to familiarize himself with the principles of Ronald Davis's work. But just by staying open and observing, not putting pressure on the child and his development, the teacher can already do a great deal for such children.

C.J.: What would you like to say to dyslexics and their parents?

M.G.: *I'd like to say one thing above all: dyslexia is not a handicap. It only becomes a problem in life if one spends years trying to acquire reading, writing and maths techniques via one's weak aspects, leaving one's real gifts untapped. If ways to use these gifts can be found in the learning process — that is, pictorial thinking and the capacity to see things from many angles — the problem can be overcome, and the dyslexic's gifts can come to full fruition.*

C.J.: Like me, you've experienced the special value of dyslexics' gifts. What opportunities do you think they will have in future?

M.G.: *Something very odd is happening in our society. The existing schooling system neglects people gifted with pictorial thinking, who have the capacity to imagine things simultaneously from several angles, because they have difficulty fitting into the prevailing mode. People who don't have these faculties get good marks and thus often also achieve higher social standing and jobs in finance or politics. But now we see the strange phenomenon that managers are sent off to expensive seminars to learn how to think pictorially — and pay £2,000 a day for the privilege! If this paradoxical situation ends through new understanding of dyslexia, as is possible through Ronald Davis's research, a great range of potential and capacities currently lacking in society will become directly available to it. In future, therefore, dyslexics will be able to find their true place with much more equanimity, and will be able to offer their gifts and talents to society.*

Learning aids

For dyslexics, 'right-hemispheric' children and as a stimulus for all who want to activate their capacity to think pictorially — a collection of ideas (with no claim to completeness):

You can find further useful suggestions on the internet at:
www.dyslexia.com/library/print/classroom.htm
'A Dyslexic Child in the Classroom. A guide for teachers and parents'

1. Clear writing on the board and on worksheets
- Writing should not be too small.
- For younger children, don't mix different writing styles.
- It should always be clear whether the letters are capitals or lower case, block letters or joined up.

Primary school worksheets — especially relating to spelling — often contain confusing mixes of letters. Often letters are distributed fairly randomly across the sheet. What is supposed to motivate children tends instead to confuse them.
- Important: Children should know from the beginning which line each of the letters belongs in.
- Discuss ascenders, descenders and size of letters.
- Short, careful handwriting exercises should be done often.
- An easily visible capital and lower-case alphabet should hang in the classroom in Class One and Two (ages six-eight) at least.

2. Clear, easily legible worksheets and reading texts
A well-presented text makes reading easier for everyone: it's easier to get a quick overview (e.g. newspaper texts).

No small font sizes! Include picture material if possible.

3. Give complete ideas/pictures at the outset
- Present clear aims.
- Overview of the theme/subject.
- Introduce any necessary words/concepts at the beginning, e.g. by making them 'visible' through symbol mastery.
- Give a printed sheet with key-word overview.
- Make a finished model (e.g. in art or handwork).
- Counting/maths: give an introductory task with example of how to solve it. Or develop tasks from the end solution.

4. Create opportunities for pupils to learn from each other
This is why it doesn't seem helpful to divide groups according to ability level. It's better to let pupils support one another.

5. When working on texts:
- Use good texts!
- First give an overview: what is the subject/theme? How is it structured? What is its external form? Key words? Names? Numbers? Any obvious punctuation?
- Exams: read out texts and where applicable have an oral exam or additional oral exam.
- Use another example to formulate an interpretation in advance of the exam.

- 'What do you see? What do you feel? What does that mean to you?'

6. Practising oral retelling the following day
- Note: dates and proper names are extremely difficult to remember, and should be written on the board.
- One should also try to link these strongly with pictorial/feeling pictures/ideas.
- Get children to relate a narrative backwards.

7. Ways of engaging creatively with learning materials
- Use your own ideas (without value judgements!)
- Be in the picture yourself.
- Include yourself in the context.
- Make mnemonics, get children to find mnemonics.
- Use mind-mapping and clustering methods.
- Make abstract ideas pictorial.
- What do you picture? What do you see? What feelings do you have about it? What does it mean? Find illustrative sentences.

8. Foreign languages
Learn vocabulary in pictorial contexts.

If translation is necessary, then get children to decode text (literal translation, cf. Birkenbihl *Fremdsprachen leicht gemacht* ['Learning languages the easy way'].

Stay in foreign countries.

9. Work materials
- Encyclopaedia (where necessary also as computer program, e.g. Encarta).
- Atlas (map of the world in classroom).
- For historical understanding: timeline or similar on classroom wall.
- Thesaurus/dictionary
- Foreign language dictionary
- For older pupils: access to the Internet.
- Audio-books
- Study of non-alphabetic scripts (e.g. hieroglyphs) or — very motivating! — the kanji trainer, a computer program for creative engagement with Japanese characters (Ingenio).

Something to ponder

'Writing's easier if I hold something in my left hand, such as the pen cap.'

'I run through the lesson backwards, then I know if I've missed something out.'

'You lose your fear of the blank sheet of paper if you first write any old thing on a piece of paper for five minutes. Afterwards, writing is easier.'

References

1. Terlouw, 160
2. Ehmann, 72
3. *Focus*, 51/94
4. Davis, *The Gift of Dyslexia*, 4
5. Reti, 77
6. Davis, *The Gift of Dyslexia*, 3-5
7. Steiner, GA 308, lecture 2: April 9, 1924
8. Davis Dyslexia Association workshop handbook, 11
9. Davis, *The Gift of Dyslexia*, 131
10. Davis, *The Gift of Dyslexia*, 131
11. Steiner, *Zur Sinneslehre*, 121
12. Steiner, *Sprechen und Sprache*, 99
13. *The Gift of Dyslexia* , 244
14. Steiner, GA 302, lecture 3: June 14, 1921
15. *The Gift of Dyslexia*, 120
16. Steiner, GA 317, lecture 1: June 25, 1924
17. Davis *The Gift of Dyslexia*, 246
18. Davis, *The Gift of Dyslexia*, 248
19. Davis, *The Gift of Dyslexia*, 81–83
20. Dühnfort/Kranich, 21
21. Steiner, *Zur Sinneslehre*, 87
22. Steiner, *Sprechen und Sprache*, 95
23. Steiner, *Sprechen und Sprache*, 24
24. Steiner, GA 306, lecture 3: April 17, 1923
25. Davis, *The Gift of Dyslexia*, 84
26. Steiner, GA 306, lecture 4: April 18, 1923
27. Steiner, GA 28, 5—6 (Autobiog)
28. Steiner, GA 28, 11
29. Steiner, GA 28, 17
30. Steiner, GA 28, 5
31. Steiner, GA 311, TB 674, lecture 2: August 13, 1924; see also TB 657, 127–130; GA 302, lecture 8: June 19, 1921, TB 648, 136–137; GA 303, lecture 7: December 29, 1921, TB 604, 96–97 and 129; GA 305, lecture 5: August 21, 1922; GA 302a, lecture 1: June 21, 1922

32. Davis, *The Gift of Dyslexia*, 133

33. Davis, *The Gift of Dyslexia*, 247

34. Steiner, GA 161, lecture 12: May 1, 1915; see also lecture 13: May 2, 1915; and GA 350, lecture 1: May 30, 1923, where Steiner likewise speaks of a sense of 'well-being' arising in thinking when one is repeatedly led back to a place of 'orientation.'

35. Davis, workshop handbook, 22

36. Steiner, GA 306, lecture 4: April 18, 1923

37. Davis, workshop handbook, 80

38. Steiner, GA 34/308

39. Steiner, GA 311, lecture 6: August 18, 1924

40. Davis, *The Gift of Dyslexia*, 241

41. Steiner, *Sprache und Sprechen*, 127

42. Steiner, hand-written addendum to GA 28 (Autobiog)

43. Steiner, GA 294, lecture 5: August 26, 1919

44. Ehmann

45. Steiner, GA 13

46. Steiner, GA 300/2: March 15, 1922

47. Steiner, GA 302, lecture 8: June 19, 1921

48. Ehmann, 70

49. Jaenicke, 232

50. *Erziehungskunst* 10/96 (German arts education magazine for Waldorf schools)

51. Terlouw, 162

52. Steiner, GA 301, answers to questions

53. Vester, *Denken, Lernen, Vergessen*, 106

54. Balhorn/Brüggemann, 103–104

55. *The Dyslexic Reader*, issue 11, 1997, 5

56. Steiner, GA 152, October 14, 1913

57. Steiner, GA 152, 129–130

58. See the publication by Herbert Seufert, 'Die schöpferischen Gestaltungskräfte — und deren Zusammenhang mit der rechten Gehirnhälfte' (The creative forces — and their connection with the right side of the brain) in *Erziehungskunst*, September 1992. See also W.E. Brown, S. Eliez, V. Menon et al: 'Preliminary evidence of widespread morphological variations of the brain in dyslexia,' in: *Neurology*, 56 (2001), 781–783; B. Horwitz, J.M. Rumsey, B.C. Donahue: 'Functional connectivity of the angular gyrus and dyslexia,' in *Neurobiology*, 95 (1998), 8939–8944; J.M. Rumsey, B. Horwitz et al: 'A functional lesion in developmental dyslexia: left angular gyral blood flow predicts severity,' in *Brain and Language*, 70 (1999), 187–204; S.E. Shaywitz, B.A. Shaywitz, R. Fulbright et al: 'Neural Systems for Compresation and Persistence: Young Adult Outcome of Childhood Reading Disability,' in *Biological Psychiatry*, 54 (2003), 25-33; P.E. Turkeltaub, L. Gareau, D.L. Flowers et al: 'Development of neural mechanisms for reading,' in *Nature Neuroscience*, 6 (2003), 767–773, 769

59. Steiner, GA 311, lecture 2: April 16, 1923

60. quoted in Edwards, 51

61. quoted in Edwards, 29

62. Vitale, 9

63. Vitale, 13

64. Edwards, 40

65. quoted in Edwards, 15

66. Steiner, GA 293, lecture 2: August 22, 1919

67. Steiner, GA 293, lecture 2: August 22, 1919

68. Steiner, GA 293, lecture 7: August 28, 1919

69. Birkenbihl, *Stroh im Kopf?*, 27

70. Birkenbihl, *Stroh im Kopf?*, 156

71. Edwards, 36–37

72. Huhn, 81

73. Huhn, 103

74. Steiner, GA 306, April 16, 1923

75. quoted in Edwards, 57

76. Steiner, GA 305, lecture 2: August 17, 1922

77. Birkenbihl, *Stroh im Kopf?*, 29

78. Holzapfel, 81

79. Steiner, GA 305, lecture 1: August 16, 1922; and GA 300/2, 300/3: May 10, 1922 and May 25, 1923

80. e.g. GA 300/1: June 14, 1920

81. McAllen, 13–14

82. Springer/Deutsch, 73, 195, 228, 240

83. Edwards, 78

84. Vitale, 107

85. Steiner, GA 301, lecture 12: May 7, 1920

86. Steiner, GA 294, lecture 7: August 28, 1919

87. Steiner, GA 305, lecture 4: August 19, 1922; also: Steiner, GA 302, lecture 4: June 15, 1921; Steiner, GA 307, lecture 5: August 6, 1923; Steiner, GA 303, lecture 16: January 7, 1922; and Steiner, GA 293, introductory address, August 20, 1919

88. Huhn, 138

89. Birkenbihl, Stroh im Kopf? 29

90. Birkenbihl, *Stroh im Kopf?* 30

91. Steiner, GA 300/1: May 26, 1921

92. Davis, *The Gift of Dyslexia*, 68

93. Steiner, GA 311, lectures 1 and 2: August 12 and 13, 1925

94. Steiner, GA 294

95. GA 294, August 25, 1919

96. Davis, *The Gift of Dyslexia*, 47

97. Vitale, 75

98. Vitale, 79

99. Vitale, 19

100. Steiner, GA 294: August 25, 1919

101. Steiner, GA 277: October 30, 1920

102. Steiner, GA 306, lecture 4: April 18, 1923; and GA 294, lecture 5: August 26, 1919

103. Aeppli; Neuffer, 191

104. Steiner, GA 305: August, 21 1922

105. Steiner, GA 296, drawing 2

106. Steiner, GA 306, lecture 3: April 17, 1923

107. Steiner, GA 294, lecture 1: August 21, 1919

108. Steiner, GA 306, lecture 3: April 17, 1923

109. Steiner, GA 306, lecture 3: April 17, 1923

110. Steiner, GA 294, lecture 5: August 26, 1919

111. Steiner, GA 311, lecture 2: August 13, 1924

112. Steiner, GA 294, lecture 5: August 26, 1919
113. Steiner, GA 303, lecture 9: December 31, 1921
114. Steiner, GA 305, lecture 5: August 21, 1922
115. Davis, *The Dyslexia Journal*, summer 1998
116. Davis, *The Gift of Dyslexia*, 202
117. Steiner, GA 143, January 11, 1912
118. Steiner, GA 294, August 21, 1919
119. Steiner, GA 294, lecture 5: August 26, 1919
120. Steiner, GA 303, lecture 9: December 31, 1921
121. Steiner, GA 303, lecture 9: December 31, 1921
122. Steiner, GA 306, April 18, 1923
123. Davis, *The Gift of Dyslexia*, 202
124. Steiner, GA 209, lecture 2: December 18, 1921
125. Steiner, GA 295, curriculum lecture 2: September 6, 1919
126. Steiner, GA 294, lecture 5: August 26, 1919
127. Ehmann, 96
128. in *Anthroposophy in Everyday Life*, SteinerBooks 1995
129. Steiner, GA 301, lecture 10: May 5, 1920
130. *Dyslexia Journal*, May 1999
131. Davis, *The Gift of Dyslexia*, 234
132. Behrendt
133. Steiner, GA 311, lecture 2: August 13, 1924
134. Steiner, GA 300/1: January 16, 1921
135. Steiner, GA 295, first curriculum lecture: September 6, 1919
136. Steiner, GA 294, lecture 10: September 1, 1919
137. Steiner, GA 294, lecture 10: September 1, 1919
138. Davis, *The Gift of Dyslexia*, 77
139. Steiner, GA 302, lecture 1: June 12, 1921
140. Steiner, GA 127, December 19, 1911
141. Aarne/Thompson
142. Davis, *The Gift of Dyslexia*, 79
143. Steiner, GA 127, December 19, 1911
144. GA 295, fifth discussion: August 26, 1919
145. Sanders, 76
146. Steiner, GA 295, first curriculum lecture: September 6, 1919
147. Davis, *The Gift of Dyslexia*, 40
148. Steiner. GA 294, lecture 5: August 26, 1919
149. Steiner, GA 294, lecture 1: August 21, 1919
150. Steiner, GA 28, 10
151. Steiner, GA 395, lecture 1: September 6, 1919
152. Steiner, GA 302, lecture 1, June 12, 1921
153. Steiner, GA 308, lecture 4: April 10, 1924
154. *Dyslexia Journal*, autumn/winter 97/98
155. Steiner, GA 295, lecture 1: September 6, 1919
156. Steiner, GA 295, discussion 6, August 27, 1919
157. Steiner, GA 295, discussion 6: August 27, 1919
158. Steiner, GA 34
159. Davis, *The Gift of Dyslexia*, 34

160. Davis, *The Gift of Dyslexia*, 64
161. Davis, workshop handbook
162. Birkenbihl, *Stroh im Kopf?* 65
163. Davis, *The Gift of Dyslexia*, 221
164. Davis, *The Gift of Dyslexia*, 221
165. Poturzyn (ed.): Wachsmuth 'The Final Years'
166. Steiner, GA 299
167. Steiner, GA 294, lecture 4: January 2, 1920
168. Dühnfort, 129–130
169. Steiner, GA 294, lecture 4: August 25, 1919
170. Gelb
171. Steiner, GA 277, address prior to a eurythmy performance: October 30, 1920
172. Steiner, GA 294, lecture 5: August 26, 1919
173. Steiner, GA 311, lecture 2: August 13, 1924
174. Steiner, GA 300/1, discussion on Monday, December 27, 1919
175. *Hamburger Abendblatt*, September 4, 1997
176. *THINK* instruction leaflet, 44
177. Edwards, 50
178. Steiner, GA 311, lecture 4: August 15, 1924
179. see Dühnfort/Kranich, 42
180. Birkenbihl, *Stichwort Schule. Trotz Schule lernen!* 56
181. Steiner, GA 311, lecture 4: August 15, 1924
182. see Dühnfort/Kranich, 36; and McAllen, 42
183. Steiner, GA 301, lecture 6: April 28, 1920
184. Davis, *The Gift of Dyslexia*, 146
185. Steiner, GA 11, lecture 4: August 15, 1924
186. Steiner,GA 301, Dornach 1991, 90
187. *The Koran,* Suras 96, 1–5
188. see Birkenbihl, *Sprachenlernen leichgemacht;* and Helms
189. Steiner, GA 300/1, 113

Bibliography

Aarne, Antti/Thompson, Stith (1961) *The Types of the Folk tales. A Classification and Bibliography.* Second Revision, Helsinki

Ayres, A. Jean (1984) *Sensory Integration and the Child.* Western Psychological Services

Aeppli, Willi (1988) *Aus dem Anfangsunterricht einer Rudolf Steiner-Schule.* Verlag Rolf Kugler, Oberwil b. Zug

Balhorn, Heiko/Brügelmann, Hans (ed.) (1995) *Rätsel des Schriftspracherwerbs. Neue Sichtweisen aus der Forschung.* Libelle Verlag, Lengwil am Bodensee

Baur, Alfred (1985) *Sprachspiele fuer Kinder. Eine heitere Hilfe zu richtigem Reden.* J. Ch. Mellinger Verlag, Stuttgart

Behrendt, Babette (1993) *Gesteigerte Lern-Ergebnisse durch Lese-Erlebnisse mit englischsprachiger Literatur: Ein neues Lehrgangmodell von H.-J. Modlmayr.* (Dortmunder Konzepte zur Fremdsprachendidaktik 2), Universitätsverlag Dr. N. Brockmeyer, Bochum

Birkenbihl, Vera F. (1997) *Stroh im Kopf? Gebrauchsanleitung fürs Gehirn.* mvg-verlag, Landsberg am Lech
—, (1997) *Stichwort Schule. Trotz Schule lernen!* mvg-verlag, Landsberg am Lech
—, (1997) *Sprachenlernen leichgemacht! Die Birkenbihl-Methode zum Fremdsprachenlernen.* mvg-verlag, Landsberg am Lech

Buzan, Tony (1991) *Speed Reading.* Plume, U.S.A.

Carlgren, Frans (2008) *Education Towards Freedom: Rudolf Steiner Education: A survey of the work of Waldorf schools throughout the world*, Floris Books, Edinburgh

Davis, Ronald D. (1997) *The Gift of Dyslexia. Why some of the brightest people can't read and how they can learn.* Souvenir Press, London
—, *The Gift of Learning* (2003) Perigee Books, U.S.A.
—, Workshop handbook (1996) Davis Dyslexia Association Deutschland

DER GROSSE DUDEN (1970) volume 10, *Bedeutungswörterbuch.* Dudenverlag, Mannheim, Vienna, Zurich

Dühnfort, Erika (1980) *Der Sprachbau als Kunstwerk. Grammatik im Rahmen der Waldorfpädagogik.* Verlag Freies Geistesleben, Stuttgart

Dühnfort, Erika / Kranich, E. Michael (1996) *Der Anfangsunterricht im Schreiben und Lesen und seine Bedeutung für das Lernen und die Entwicklung des Kindes.* Verlag Freies Geistesleben, Stuttgart

Ehmann, Hermann (1995) *Ist mein Kind Legastheniker? Ein Ratgeber zur Lese- und Rechtschreibschwäche.* C.H. Beck-Verlag, Munich

Edwards, Betty (1993) *Drawing on the Right Side of the Brain.* Harper Collins, London

Friedenthal, Richard (1963) *Goethe. Sein Leben und seine Zeit.* Deutscher Bücherbund, Stuttgart

Gabert, Erich (1963) *Verzeichnis der Äußerungen Rudolf Steiners. Über den Grammatik-Unterricht.* Photocopied manuscript issued by the Bund der freien Waldorfschulen, Stuttgart

Gelb, Michael J. (1998) *Das Leonardo-Prinzip; Die sieben Schritte zum Erfolg.* vgs Verlagsgesellschaft, Cologne

Gebser, Jean (1986) *Ursprung und Gegenwart,* vols 2–4 of the complete edition, Novalis Verlag AG, Schaffhausen

Hartmann, Thom (1996) *Beyond ADD: Hunting for Reasons in the Past and Present.* Underwood Books

Haberland, Gerhard (1995) *Leserechtschreibeschwäche? Rechenschwäche? Weder Schwäche noch Defizit! Ein Leitfaden zur Hilfe und Selbsthilfe für Lehrer und Eltern betroffener Kinder*

Holtzapfel, Walter (1966) *Kinderschicksale, Entwicklungsrichtungen.* Verlag am Goetheanum, Dornach (Switzerland)

Huhn, Gerhard, *Kreativität und Schule. Risiken derzeitigen Lehrpläne für die freie Entfaltung der Kinder. Verfassungswidrigkeit staatlicher Regelungen von Bildungszielen und Unterrichtsinhalten vor dem Hintergrund neuerer Erkenntnisse aus der Gehirnforschung.* VWB-Verlag für Wissenschaft und Bildung, Synchron Verlag, Berlin

Helms, Wilfried, *Vokabeln lernen — 100% behalten* (in the 'Mind unlimited series'). Can be ordered from Wilfried Helms, Forsthausstr. 56, 35043 Marburg

Jaenicke, Hans Friedbert (1996) *Kinder mit Entwicklungsstörungen.* Verlag Freies Geistesleben, Stuttgart

Köhler, Henning (1997) *'Schwierige' Kinder gibt es nicht. Plädoyer für eine Umwandlung des pädagogischen Denkens.* Verlag Freies Geistesleben, Stuttgart

McAllen, Audrey (1990) *The Extra Lesson.* Robinswood Press, Stourbridge

Neuffer, Helmut (ed.) (1997) *Zum Unterricht des Klassenlehrers an der Waldorfschule.* Verlag Freies Geistesleben, Stuttgart

Poturzyn, M.J. Krück v. (ed.) (1956) *Wir erlebten Rudolf Steiner.* Verlag Freies Geistesleben, Stuttgart

Reti, Ladislao (ed.) (1979) *Leonardo — Künstler, Forscher, Magier.* Fischer-Verlag

Rico, L. Gabriele (1998) *Garantiert schreiben lernen. Sprachliche Kreativität methodisch entwickeln — ein Intensivkurs.* Rowohlt Verlag, Reinbeck

Sheldrake, Rupert (1995) *The Presence of the Past. Morphic Resonance and the Habits of Nature.* Park Street Press, Vermont

Sanders, Barry (1995) *A is for Ox: The Collapse of Literacy and the Rise of Violence in an Electronic Age.* Vintage, London

Sacks, Oliver (1996) *An Anthropologist on Mars: Seven Paradoxical Tales.* Vintage, London

Saint-Exupery, Antoine de (2007) *The Little Prince.* Heritage

Springer, Sally P. / Deutsch, Georg (2001) *Left Brain, Right Brain: Perspectives from Cognitive Neuroscience.* W.H. Freeman, U.S.A.

Steltzer, Saskia (1998) *Wenn die Wörter tanzen. Legasthenie und Schule.* Ariston Verlag, Munich

Steiner, Rudolf, (1995) *Anthroposophy in Everyday Life,* Anthroposophic Press, Massachusetts
—, (2006) *Approaching the Mystery of Golgotha,* GA (Gesamtausgabe/Complete Works) 152, SteinerBooks, Massachusetts
—, (2006) *Autobiography,* GA 28, SteinerBooks, Massachusetts
—, (2007) *Balance in Teaching,* GA 302a, SteinerBooks, Massachusetts
—, (1996) *The Child's Changing Consciousness,* GA 306, Anthroposophic Press, Massachusetts
—, (1997) *Discussions with Teachers,* GA 295, Anthroposophic Press, Massachusetts
—, (1996) *Education for Adolescents,* GA 302, Anthroposophic Press, Massachusetts
—, (1998) *Education for Special Needs,* GA 317, Rudolf Steiner Press, England
—, (1996) *The Education of the Child,* GA 34, Anthroposophic Press, Massachusetts
—, (1983) *Erfahrungen des Übersinnlichen. Die Wege der Seele zu Christus,* GA 143, Rudolf Steiner Verlag, Dornach
—, (1997) *The Essentials of Education,* GA 308, Anthroposophic Press, Massachusetts

—, (2007) *Eurythmy: an Introductory Reader,* Rudolf Steiner Press, England

—, (1980) *Eurythmie. Die Offenbarung der sprechenden Seele,* GA 277, Rudolf Steiner Verlag, Dornach

—, (1998) *Faculty Meetings with Rudolf Steiner,* GA 300, Anthroposophic Press, Massachusetts

—, (1996) *The Foundations of Human Experience,* GA 293, Anthroposophic Press, Massachusetts

—, (2000) *From Mammoths to Mediums,* GA 350, Rudolf Steiner Press, England

—, (1995) *The Genius of Language,* GA 299, Anthroposophic Press, Massachusetts

—, (1994) *How to Know Higher Worlds,* GA 10, Anthroposophic Press, Massachusetts

—, (1995) *Kingdom of Childhood, The,* GA 311, Anthroposophic Press, Massachusetts

—, (1981) *Man as a Being of Sense and Perception,* GA 206, Steiner Book Centre, Vancouver

—, (1975) *Die Mission der neuen Geistesoffenbarung,* GA 127, Rudolf Steiner Verlag, Dornach

—, (2004) *A Modern Art of Education,* GA 307, SteinerBooks, Massachusetts

—, (1982) *Nordische und mitteleuropäische Geistimpulse,* GA 209, Rudolf Steiner Verlag, Dornach

—, (1997) *An Outline of Esoteric Science,* GA 13 Anthroposophic Press, Massachusetts

—, (1999) *The Philosophy of Freedom,* GA 4, Rudolf Steiner Press, England

—, (2000) *Practical Advice to Teachers,* GA 294, SteinerBooks, Massachusetts

—, (2001) *The Renewal of Education through the Science of the Spirit,* GA 301, SteinerBooks, Massachusetts

—, (1996) *Rudolf Steiner in the Waldorf School,* GA 298, Anthroposophic Press, Massachusetts

—, (2003) *Soul Economy Body, Soul, and Spirit in Waldorf Education,* GA 303, SteinerBooks, Massachusetts

—, (2004) *The Spiritual Ground of Education,* GA 305, SteinerBooks, Massachusetts

—, (1989) *Sprechen und Sprache,* (Ed. C. Lindenberg), Verlag Freies Geistesleben, Stuttgart

—, (1990) *Wandtafelzeichnungen zum Vortragswerk,* Rudolf Steiner Verlag, Dornach

—, (1980) *Wege der geistigen Erkenntnis und der Erneuerung künstlerischer Weltanschauung,* GA 161, Rudolf Steiner Verlag, Dornach

—, (1994) *Zur Sinneslehre,* (Ed. C. Lindenberg), Verlag Freies Geistesleben, Stuttgart

Temple, Robin (1999) *Legasthenie und Begabung. Ronald D. Davis und traditionelle Methoden. Ein Vergleich.* Ariston Verlag

Terlouw, Moniek (1995) *Legasthenie und ihre Behandlung.* Verlag Freies Geistesleben, Stuttgart

The Ladybird Key Word Reading Scheme, Ladybird Books Ltd., Loughborough, Leicestershire

Vester, Frederic (1991) *Denken, Lernen, Vergessen. Was geht in unserem Kopf vor, wie lernt das Gehirn, und wann lässt es uns im Stich?* dtv, Munich

—, *Visuelle Weltgeschichte der alten Kulturen (Sehen, Staunen, Wissen* series). Gerstenberg Verlag, Hildesheim

Vitale, Barbara Meister (1982) *Unicorns Are Real. A Right-Brained Approach to Learning.* Pro-Ed, Austin, Texas

Education Towards Freedom

Rudolf Steiner Education: A survey of the work of Waldorf Schools throughout the world

Frans Carlgren

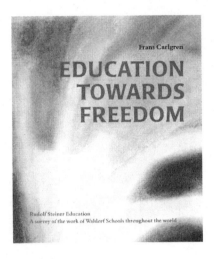

Education Towards Freedom was first published in 1976, and since then has sold over ten thousand copies in English. When it appeared, there were around 100 Steiner-Waldorf schools throughout the world; now there are almost 1000.

During this time, Steiner-Waldorf education has become increasingly known in the mainstream, and increasingly valued for its alternative approaches to children's learning and development. The great breadth and richness of the approach is what has attracted so many parents to its schools and books like *Education Towards Freedom* have helped them make the informed choice to take a different route for their children.

The book covers all aspects of Steiner-Waldorf education and divides it into the pre-school years, the first eight years (starting about age seven), and the last four years (from 14 to 18). There are also sections on the rhythm of the day, specific subjects, the use of textbooks, and school in the modern world.

www.florisbooks.co.uk

Steiner Education in Theory and Practice

Gilbert Childs

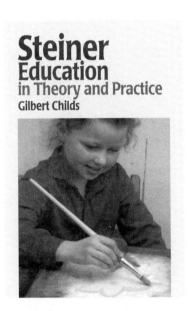

This is a detailed account of Rudolf Steiner's view of children, and the role education must play in their successful development.

Gilbert Childs examines and explains the curriculum of Steiner-Waldorf schools, showing how their unique teaching practices take a holistic view of the child. He looks particularly at issues such as creativity, imagination, and intellect, and how the schools try to produce rounded, responsible young adults.

He concludes that our approach to the education of our children is an issue of the utmost urgency for the future of our society.

www.florisbooks.co.uk